Ponderings
With Roy & Irv

by Doug Rucker

Ponderings
by Doug Rucker

Copyright © 2023 Doug Rucker
All Rights Reserved

Vilimandyedpubco
RuckerDoug@gmail.com

No part of this publication may be reproduced, distributed, or copied in any form or by any means, including photocopying, recording, or other electronic or mechanical methods, without the prior written permission of the publisher, except in the case of brief quotations embodied in critical reviews and certain other noncommercial uses permitted by copyright law.

For permission requests, sales to U.S. bookstores and wholesalers, or to inquire about quantity discounts, please contact the publisher by email.

Library of Congress Control number 2022919538

ISBN 978-1-7354717-5-4

First Edition
10 9 8 7 6 5 4 3 2 1

Printed in the United States of America

Ponderings
With Roy & Irv

Contents

Prologue 1
Disparities. 5
He Writes 9
Unopenable Box 11
What I Like and Don't Like 13
It Don't Matter 18
Automatic Writing 22
We're Made of Colors. 24
Strong Wind and Rain. 26
Nighttime – Dream - #1 30
Nighttime – Dream - #2 32
No Life After Death 35
Why is There Water?. 39
Nighttime – Dream - #3 42
Clock Ticking Away 43
Anthropomorphism and the Serious Architect 45
When I Was a Boy 47
God's Awful Truth. 49
Topsy-Turvy Design 51
Life After Death 54
Blazondon or Hick-up High? 57
Early in the Afternoon. 60
Nighttime – Dream - #4 63
I Lay There Pondering 68
Another American. 73
Dreams and Desires 76
Suck it Up! 82
Mars and Me 84
Trapped Feelings. 85
Nighttime – Dream - #5 89
To Whom Am I Swearing 91
I Am a Leaf. 95
How to Understand the Universe 97
Beginning of Aside 101

Family Issue 103
Reliable Cosmic Conditions 106
Cosmic and Human Truth at Odds 107
   Except Humans 107
   Another Single Theory 110
Baby Doug's Near-Death Experience 113
Awareness 119
Earth's Timeline 122
What I Believe 124
More Reliable Cosmic Conditions 129
Poem 131
Laundry and Philosophy 133
How Long Will the Afterlife Last? 135
Whole Brain Living 137
I'm Stuck With Myself and Can't Get Off 138
Dream Flying Over Desert 140
Retaining Myself After Leaving My Body 143
Shadow Life 146
Shadow Life Over a Year Later 149
Dream With Long Wire 151
Another Recent Episode 153
A Frank Philosophy 154
Thinking the Whole 156
Bigger Than the Bug 157
   Talking to the Bug 158
   To Be an Architect 159
Will Humans Agree? 160
Easy Things 163
   The Universal Force 164
   No Life After Death 165
   Serious Prayer 167
   Unserious Prayer 168
Remembrances of My Father 170
There is so Much More 172
   From Lili's Last Letter 172
Black Clouds and Lightning 174

Meaning 175
On the Subject of Religion 177
   Beginning 179
   The Religion of Common Sense 179
   Common Sense Religion 180
   Commandments 181
   Ten Commandments 181
   Interpretation 183
   More Commandments 184
   Man as Species 185
   Greatest Adventures 188
   Knowing and Believing 188
   A Percentage Kind of a Guy 189
   People are Different 189
   Following Parents Beliefs 190
   Beginning of the World 190
   Process and Context 192
   Time and Reality 192
   Correct Me if I'm Wrong 193
   The Brain as Tool 193
   I See the World This Way 194
Self 195
About the Author 199
Other Books by Doug Rucker 201

Prologue

As I write this, it's July 1, 2022, which means I have lived 94 years and 179 days. Isn't that a gas?

The only thing I can even think to write about is myself. As I'd boast years ago, *"Ego as big as the whole outdoors, over the canyon rim it soars."* It looks like that might also be true for today,

If I write about my three kids it puts me at the risk of being judgmental. *(Or is that just an excuse?)* I could write about my new wife, Marge, or my parents, or my divorced wife, as dubious as I am about that episode, or life on earth or tales of the cosmos or quantum physics, about which after years of study, I know nothing.

In any case, this period of time, with the earth's fresh water evaporating, animals and people birthing and dying and the Covid-19 disease enslaving the world, this is a special time.

These days are marked to get everyone's attention; we are at a hallmark point, a marker in the history of time, a position in which it is necessary to look - or die - but not only a world-turning point but my personal turning point. I might ask the turning point to where? I'd say after living well over 94 years, a turning point to old age and death. I feel the body quietly adapting to its final resting place. One of peace and tranquility, for what else is this feeling of approaching death?

What didn't help was a recent dream that might be called a premonition or acknowledgement of a future that to me embodies an urge to listen carefully.

In a that dream, like *Little Red Riding Hood*, but not to grandmothers' house was I to go, I'm following a wide, yellow path over the hills and through the woods, past deserts, along the shore, between the trees, and while moving along what looks like a well-assigned path, I instantly wake up! I'm suddenly conscious! I'm no longer part of a dream, but awake and blatantly confronted with instant life. I was surprised! The dream had no conclusion! There was no end, no finality, just marching along the path, going, going, going, and then I woke up! The path kept going, but I had stopped.

What does it mean when a dream moves easily along, then mid-stride it stops and I awake? What does it symbolize in my life? I can't help looking inward and ask what's going on here? Does it suggest my life has been moving agreeably along and has suddenly reached the end? Quickly awakening to a symbol of my own demise astounded me. I was surprised in never before having considered such a daring occurrence! It forced me to examine life!

Since my retirement from architecture, my social accomplishments have been my writing over 30 books, dealing with the agony of my wife, Marge, dying, and showing my own photos in over 150 art shows, culminating in a 52-piece, one-man show at the Malibu Civic Center, introduced by Jefferson Wagner, Malibu's Mayor. I also just finished a book called *Poetries*, with a new book called *Catchall* now being printed. In my physical health the future is uncertain. I'm 94 years old with an ever-worsening body physically plodding through its relentless path. Though in the dream, as also in reality, the pathway might continue to eternity, but I do not follow. Awakening with creative thoughts tells me, *enough of this kind of thinking,*

The dream says I have stopped, but the health of my body and reality shows me I have not stopped. Dreams are dreams and reality is real. A dream may foretell one thing, but life may be foretelling another. I haven't actually died! I'm still living. The question sitting on the fence like a crow imagining a full stomach is what I'm to do with lagging energy now that my writing, artwork, architecture, marriages and raising my children are just about over.

I was reading a book about what to write about. The conclusion was, *"Tell the people what you want them to know."* That's a subject that sometimes lies quiet in this, my later life. I suppose I could tell them about what I am presently reading. Would that be fun? Is that worthwhile? Something that would make my present life sit up and say, *"Howdy!"* OK! I'm reading a book about the cosmos titled *Your Place in the Universe,* by Paul M. Sutter.

But Sutter's place, your place and my place are all different. I know nothing of your life and only a little of Sutter's. The tail of other's lives is not mine to tell. What I have to tell is mine. Perhaps I'll just quote a copy of what *my editor has written on the back of my book.*

"Doug Rucker's latest, and perhaps final opus, is a touching, thoughtful, and often-humorous compilation of "found" essays and poems about life, aging, the universe and the meaning of it all, presented as a lively conversation between old friends."

Disparities

Irv
What are you going to write about?
Roy
I don't know!
Irv
Are you some kind of idiot?
Roy
Yeah!
Irv
Why aren't you smart?
Roy
I guess I'm just stupid.
Irv
You sure as hell are!
Roy
You don't have to be so agreeable!
Irv
I've got to get some thought out of you, don't I?
Roy
No, you don't!
Irv
Yes, I do!
Roy
I was born stupid.
Irv
I can see that.
Roy
I can't think of anything to write about.
Irv
Why don't you try to write something smart?
Roy
The honey doesn't fall far from the bee.
Irv
How did you learn that?

Roy
I read it in a book.
Irv
I didn't know you read books. What did the book say?
Roy
It says while the bee is flying around carrying all the honey sometimes he drops it and it falls on the ground. That means the honey doesn't fall far from the bee.
Irv
Doesn't that statement carry something more with it?
Roy
What?
Irv
Like the apple doesn't fall far from the tree, or the duck doesn't go far from the water, or the cars are still in the garage?
Roy
Hell! I don't know. Don't hang me, man! Are you trying to get me to think, or something?
Irv
I don't think I'm having that much success.
Roy
We live in a violent universe, and though it's in control of itself, it's not in control of human beings!
Irv
That sounds smart! What do you mean humans aren't in control?
Roy
If we got the money, we can go to the store and buy something, but we can't control the wind – which is part of the universe!
Irv
Wow! That's great news! How about that? We can't control the wind. Hell! I wanted to control the wind, too! Can you say something else smart?

Roy
Among many, many, many other things we can't control earthquakes, tsunamis, hurricanes, global warming, increasing temperature, the whirling of the planet and other stuff.
Irv
Shiiit! We can't?
Roy
Or even the outcome of the human species, or all non-human matter, or even the growing heat of the Earth.
Irv
OK! I'm smart enough now! So, where does that leave Heaven?
Roy
Up da creek!
Irv
Ya vol, Herr Director!
Roy
I want my life to include intelligence and humor. The above conversation is intended to have a humorous finish, because the full acknowledgement of our planet's serious condition leaves me feeling depressed and desperate. But despite that feeling, there still remain miracles in the world, like beauty, love, passion, growth and humor; that the eternal opposites discussed later in this memoir, like yes and no, love and hate, birth and death, good and bad are positive conditions that must be acknowledged. Only those living creatures that know the difference between the above can make a positive difference. At this time, humans are the only beings aware of the extent of the universe that can care. UFOs' benefits, so far, are just a waste of time. That's why living things, such as human beings who can care, are so important.
Isn't that a corker?

That reminds me of other writing attempts I've made since my last, if you'll pardon the expression, *"book."* In those I had purpose. In this effort I'm trusting I have something to say. To experience fresh air, I must go outside. But in looking at what I've written in the past and trying to keep an open mind, I see the following fits the empty bill. It's called *He Writes*.

He Writes!

He writes!

    He sits with full stomach
    Urgent against his belt.

A bulk!
A hulk!

    A regular Mickey Markum
    Who thinks with his brain. *(In Vain!)*

Rubbery, sticky matter slumps,
Tired against his cranium bone.

    He mopes in the mildest of hopes
    For a glimmer, a flicker,
    Or even a warm spot
    In his jelly of thoughts
    That might hold promise
    For a thought to be thunk.

Or a thunk to be thinked

    Or a think to be thank.

He sat, was fat, and thunk.

    Brain lost as wood,
    He thinks and stinks,
    He thank and stank)

Hopeless!

    Dead and forgotten.

Rotten!

Let us pray.

Irv
Maybe you ought to quit while you're ahead.
Roy
I would, but my body won't let me.
Irv
Your body is controlling you?
Roy
It's a funny idea, but yes, my body is not telling me to stop.
Irv
There's something really wrong here!
Roy
Wait! Wait! Something in my brain's twitching. It's a book called *Catchall* and it's whispering about things worth keeping and when I ask what? It replies with another of my poeticized compositions that may be appropriate. It's called *Unopenable Box*.
Irv
That sounds good, though it may be bad!
Roy
So offa ma haid ahma gonna risk a-printin' it.

Unopenable Box

There once was a guy named Kirk
who had been concerned about a
box that could not be opened.

    Being inoperable, it denied everyone
    the knowledge of what was inside.

Questions like, what was there
before the Big Bang? Or how did
consciousness arise? Or why can't
some animals see color? If the interior
of the box held those answers and
was unable to be opened, our
curiosity could never be quelled.

    Let's imagine Kirk sitting upright
    on a straight-backed metal chair.
    He's in his Saturday clothes on a
    concrete patio beneath a wooden
    trellis, over which is growing
    wisteria and other flowering vines.

At 35 years old, he'd been
contemplating the cosmos for
about two hours but was finally
nodding off in a welcome nap.

Within 10 minutes of falling asleep, his
body assumed a more rigid position.

    The molecules in his body had
    coagulated and forced his figure
    into a more solid position. A half-
    hour into sleep, his heart had

stopped and his blood had lost its
color and thickened to a rigid state.

In another 30 minutes, his internal
organs solidified and bonded to the bone,
and later his arms merged to his remaining
sides and the rest of his body had taken
on the appearance of a 3ft x 3ft x 3ft iron cube.

Inside this solid body-box remained an
open area of space 2ft x 2ft x 2ft. His body
molecules had been significantly reduced in
size. They'd turned into atoms with protons,
neutrons and electrons now whirling around
and around in a restless, agitated way. In
fact, in a quantum way, his body-box reached
strength beyond that of steel.

Kirk had become the unopenable box.

Irv
So, what does this have to do with anything?
Roy
Maybe I should start with, *What I Like and Don't Like.*
I ran across an essay I'd written many years ago. The
following is part of it.

What I Like and Don't Like

My family: *I love my wife, offspring & extended family and they love me.*
My work: *I am passionate about writing and photography.*
My favorite possessions: *my computer and camera.*
Words I live by: *notice the miracle of each day.*
I can't live without: *my brain.*
I am most proud of: *my deceased wife and family.*
I am inspired by: *imaginative writing and pictures.*
What keeps me awake at night: *new ideas for writing and photos.*
If I could be totally wild: *I would shock the world and myself by writing my ideas and making pictures.*
I am guilty of: *Staying in bed too long.*
One thing I never want to do again: *get bit by a dog.*
Right now I'm reading: *searching for J. D. Salinger by Ian Hamilton.*
The one thing that has changed my life: *meeting and marrying my best friend and loving companion and departed wife, Marge.*
Favorite website: *Google.*
The most important thing I ever lost: *physical flexibility and prowess.*
My best friend says: *I am a good person.*
I still can't get the hang of: *paginating books.*
The world would be a better place if: *there were fewer people and more education.*
Something most people don't know about me: *I sang in a professional chorus group at the Pasadena Playhouse theater for a month. We were in the Gilbert and Sullivan musical called The Gondoliers. I sang in the chorus and quartet in the Santa Monica Community Theater called "Girl Crazy," and did a month of chorus work in a professional performance in the Los Angeles section of*

city called Downey of Verdi's "Rigoletto."

Plays and dancing: *during that period of time when I was married to my first wife, Karon, we were members of a Renaissance Singing group that met weekly for 9 years. Afterward with my second wife, Marge, we attended a weekly improvisational dancing group for 12 years.*

The worst idea I ever had: *making a collage for an art gallery with "touching" as the theme. After a week, I threw the whole bloody mess in the trash.*

Because I loved to run: *I did so on a daily basis including 20 or so 10K or 15K races and ran from 2 to 4 miles a day for over 50 years.*

Whose diary would you most like to read: *Paul Klee's.*

Best one-liner you ever heard: *"I don't want to belong to any club that would have me as a member!" by Groucho Marx.*

At the end of a long day, the first thing I want to do is: *hit the sack.*

Always: *eat peanut butter sandwiches.*

Never: *try to paint a house with a toothbrush.*

Irv
Do you feel better now that you've got that off our chest?
Roy
It's significant only if it means I've used up a couple of pages of space and am a little closer to the end.
Irv
It sounds like you're a little obsessed with yourself.
Roy
This is an autobiography! What do you expect? Should I be talking about you?
Irv
No! No! Forget it!
Roy
I've got something else I want to say.

In studying the Universe, I've come to the conclusion there are four main points to keep in mind before we conclude anything. By the way, the cosmos is so complex we can't arrive at any truly cosmic conclusions because we're not smart enough. So I'd have to use the phrase, conclude *to the best of our ability.*
Irv
I'm not sure I'm smart enough to understand what you're saying.
Roy
You probably aren't! To understand the universe, there are four symbols, yes, no, maybe and other. While yes and no have inflexible meanings, the maybe category includes percentages between 0% and 100%. Other means *I Don't Know,* including the why, how or when of everything. Why are we here? I don't know! How do new ideas begin? I don't know! When was awareness first obtained? I don't know! Why do we sing songs? I don't know! How did consciousness arrive? I don't know! When did we know we were not perfect?
I don't know.
Irv
Ah? I'm notta sure I-aa get-aa . . .
Roy
In thinking about the *Unopenable Box* poem, it's in the category of the other, meaning we don't know how a man could turn into an unopenable box. All living things, including poisons, germs and viruses are also included in the other area because we don't know how they came about, either. They have questions few are able to answer. For starters, how could a Universe, especially one so huge, with no quantifiable dimensions, begin from nothing? Nothing else does that. How did matter of which we are made become aware with memory, sight, hearing, touch, taste and smells and the ability to plan for the future? What and where and why is the obvious

organism, the body, that goes by the name of self? We can visualize a not openable box that tells us we are the result of that of which we will never know. And likewise, we have no knowledge of how we got here nor does it seem we ever will.

Irv
Huh?

Roy
Well? Of course, there probably are future invaders from outer space and they may know. But until we can sit down with them, have a beer, and ask them, *"Hey! How did we living beings get here?"* we'll never know.

Irv
I'll never know that's for sure.

Roy
Calling aliens invaders doesn't do them justice. If they're smart enough to get here, they're smart enough to exist without planet overpopulation, to go faster than the speed of light and to not allow their species to commit suicide.

Irv
Dummkopf!!!

Roy
Having already written numerous items found wandering about in my brain, sometimes they stop and I get writer's block. I'm stuck for a subject to keep me occupied. Oh, I have lots of things to write about, but it helps to have a spark of enthusiasm. Writer's block brings up the idea of examining that blocked area to see how it got that way. What comes to mind is a title called, *It Don't Matter!*

Irv
What's that?

Roy
It Don't Matter! You might ask why the title wouldn't be *It Doesn't Matter?* It could be. It's grammatically correct and means the same, but I think not catchy enough. It's not my intent merely to be grammatical. I enjoy things

wild. Wild means any subject including dense, brainless or dim-witted, but for this new writing, does it really matter?

Irv
Let's see that paper! Can I take it home to read?

Roy
Certainly! Later I'll ask you, *"Did you read the book?"* And you'll say:

Irv
I didn't get to it yet.

Roy
It don't matter! What you see is what you get! Face reality! *It Doesn't Matter, It Don't Matter.* It Doesn't Matter! It was then I started to think I could write a book about things that don't matter. There are a lot of conversations or stories that don't matter, but in another way they're all I've got to write about. In the long run it doesn't matter! A new essay follows that doesn't matter. It's entitled, *It Don't Matter.*

It Don't Matter

We live in a rural area about four miles from the ocean in an isolated community at about 1,800 feet above sea level. After brunch, my wife, Marge, and I went for a walk with her son, Chris, and his college-age daughter, Morgan. The four of us went down the narrow paved street to Vera Lane, then left past a neighbor's house distinguished by a black-trunked oak tree with powerful limbs brazen and strong, silhouetted against a cerulean sky.

Irv
What's cerulean?
Roy
Bluish! Forget it!

Then, across the old wooden bridge built at the turn of the century where we stopped. Chris and I, rigid and stalwart, looked to the left. Marge and Morgan, slim and beautiful, looked to the right. In the vicinity we saw the bottom of a shallow stream, dark and babbling between burned-broken logs and half-soaked boulders, plus, I assume, a few snakes, frogs, lizards and crickets.

We made our way beneath live oaks and down the narrow street bordering a darkened hillside with ancient sycamores on the creek side and oaks on the mountainside, and we strolled under dappling shade, soothing to our nerves and made forgettable small talk.

Presently, the towering trees ended and we emerged from the shadows to a sunny sky, and a place where the road ends and the closed privacy gate begins with a metal sign wired to a chain-link gate, containing the surprising announcement, *Be Well!*

This was the place to end our journey, a place to turn back and retrace our steps. The hills across the valley were glowing yellow-brown, the sky a deep, overpowering blue, while the diligent sun plunged its relentless rays into the darkening canyon.

Back up the hill, where the trees and waterfall began, Marge told us a story, the substance of which is another tale.

Yes! We made it home all right!

Irv
Why did you insert the It Don't Matter name of the story above, even though I don't think it's going to break any records for storytelling?
Roy
Because the story doesn't matter and I have nothing else to say. At least the little story is something.
Irv
Do you think the story has anything going for it?
Roy
Well, as I see it it's like a little poem, even though it's written like a dialogue from one idiot about a subject leading us to believe it is of absolutely no consequence whatever. It's suitably entitled, *It Don't Matter,* agreeing exactly with what it means. But then it could be interpreted as a vignette about our somewhat boring life in Southern California.
Irv
Is that something that should occur at this particular place in the book?
Roy
If the sole purpose in writing this text is an attempt to have enough words and thoughts to fill a book, and I

haven't the foggiest idea of how to do that, at least this is one desperate attempt.
Irv
Do you like it?
Roy
Yes and no! It could be worse!
Irv
How's that?
Roy
First, the story is true. My beautiful wife, now dead for almost five years, and I did go for a walk with her beloved son, Chris, and his remarkable daughter, Morgan, the then 18-year-old college student. Second, if I didn't include the story about her, the incidence of this unique episode and special intimate family memoir would be totally inaccurate and lost in the annals of some overlooked and outdated computer or long-forgotten notebook.
Irv
That brings up the question: Should things be written down to contemplate another day?
Roy
I think so.
Irv
Until now I never thought of it that way. At least I know a teeny bit more about the less important actions of ineffective lives.
Roy
Yes, that's right, and is not knowledge power?
Irv
I'm not sure how much this additional knowledge makes me feel more powerful than I felt before. I guess I feel just a wee bit more powerful than before, but I'm not sure powerful is the word for it. What's next?

Roy
I think I'll rifle through my short collection and yank out something probably totally unrelated to anything of true consequence in God's Great Universe.
Irv
I can't wait.
Roy
I just found something I thought I'd lost. How about *Automatic Writing?*

Automatic Writing

It has been one of my philosophies that if anyone writes a jumble of words until they have reached the amount to fill a book then the reader if any, would know more than he might care to know about the writer.

What would the writer learn? He might learn about himself. Or he might not. It depends on whether he is motivated to learn about himself or not. What is it about motivation? Motivation seems to be the hardest thing by which to come. It's difficult to be motivated.

What motivates people anyway? Motivation is more important than what is produced. If one is motivated one will produce anything, but whether or not it will be worthwhile needs appraising.

I might be motivated to buy an ice cream cone. A really big one! A triple-decker rocky road with chocolate sauce, ground nuts, whipped cream and cherry on top!

But still, what motivates my desire for a cone? Hunger, of course. Not *real* hunger, but a *sort-of* hunger. Not hunger for a reasonable life like in the depressed cities of Bangladesh, but more of a hunger of the rich. I'm not sure hunger is the proper word. Perhaps, *wimpy-little-kinda-wanna-sorta-hankerin-for-a-little-extra*, might be the proper word – or words.

I might want a chocolate cone, but now I'm far from discussing serious motivation. Einstein was motivated to discover E=MC squared. I don't think I will discover anything like E=MC squared particularly since I got a D in Physics.

Irv
Well, that's an essay to which I can't connect. It has purpose, meaning, and philosophic and psychic ideas, something to which only meaning can subscribe.

Roy
I don't even like that essay. I put it in here to take up space. Try the next one on for size. It will knock your socks off! Take off your hat, it's *We're Made of Colors*.

We're Made of Colors

What if instead of myself being made of a skin color I was made of different colors? Different colors usually provoke the same feelings in everyone. Since each day of my existence is different, so would my colors be different. Different colors would match different moods I felt in my body. If I were sad, I might be a simple color like soft gray. If later I heard good news, my picture might brighten by the gentle addition of white or yellow. If driving a car and I accidently bumped another and gave us each fender benders I'd display shock or fright and my color might briefly change to the sharper red of panic with a splash of yellow and a jagged blotch of black for despair.

If I were made of colors, people would more clearly see my moods and know whether I was happy or sad or bored with my whole being and longing for a nap, or hundreds of in-between moods and tempers including significant or indescribable augmentations. And then:

Were I a dancer, I'd dance the dance of each new color! If today I have four elements, black, red, blue and light blue, then *black is* the symbol of power, strength and mystery; *red,* is the sign of blood, fire and passion; *blue,* signifies depth, expertise and stability; and *light blue,* expresses peacefulness, reliability and tranquility. While dancing colored shapes, the lines of my body and depending on talent, would be all over the place with some sense of rhythm, harmony and purpose.

My personal picture would boil down to one of *strength, passion, stability and tranquility.* Wouldn't that be the cat's meow?

Roy
The above is a discussion about people with strong feelings outwardly expressed as an intensity of colors, but sometimes rarely discussed because of the impossibility of people to express emotions they feel in color. If a person were sitting looking straight at you with a normal expression on his face, and inside he or she was a raging inferno of conflicted passion, his or her face wouldn't match what he or she was feeling inside and they'd be sending off the conflicting messages; jagged red, knifing yellow, an explosion of white with smaller triangles of blue, green and chartreuse. A normal responder could be easily forgiven by reacting to a face of colors rather than the more passionate emotions less explicitly expressed.

Irv
So what does this have to do with the price of eggs?

Roy
Nothing, just a psychological idea that usually ends up unworthy of expression due to the lack of any reasonable outcome it might embrace. It would be sort of like throwing trash into a raging stream.

Irv
Well, that beats my whole card! What's next?

Roy
I thought this very book needs a poem.

Irv
Why's that?

Roy
I like poems and try to write one if I can think of one.

Irv
Do we have any choice?

Roy
Yeah, that or nothing. It's called *Strong Wind and Rain*.

Irv
OK! If I have to listen, I will.

Strong Wind and Rain

Huddling inside, Marge and I
and other restless partygoer's
heard impacts from different
lightening strikes thrashing in
the forests of the planet, some
closer, some farther away.

      Howling through the trees,
      the rain-driven wind increased.
      Tent material bowed and
      billowed and alternatively
      collapsed, then suddenly pulled
      against restraining ropes.

As in a dream, branches,
bent their zany way and
snapped and whipped in
the force and power of the
gale. Twigs and leaves rattled
and blew into nowhere.

      In the vast forest the clatter of
      branches in the tops of trees were
      piercing as they slammed into one
      another. Leaves were torn from
      stems and resembled dark clouds
      when masses of them were seen high
      in the sky flickering to nowhere.

Others with firm stems from
countless years of frightening winds,
rattled and scrabbled and stubbornly
remained in their places, and because

of the clamor, sometimes ear-piercing
wind made talking unintelligible.

> In fact, communication was utterly
> impossible. My own voice could
> not have been heard over the force
> of the gale. The human group assumed a low
> posture on the platform, while the torrential
> storm persisted on course.

Hours passed, and the group and
I remained in stillness. With time
interminable, frequent bombings
of lightning lessened, being farther
away and at last, perhaps five
or six hours later, the wind finally
died and the atmosphere became
lethargic.

> On leathery stems, the
> large, poplar shaped leaves
> were quietly exhausted,
> having been severely blown
> and put to the test
> they appeared forlorn.

I gazed at the staging area. Debris
was dangling from walls and
roofs. Slim pieces of wood from
stricken sides of higher buildings
littered the platform. Detritus from
decks and drifts of dust and dirt, piles

> of leaves and small branches, were
> strewn over the display area.
> After a short period, a few human creatures

quietly opened their apartment windows, and soft whispering and inarticulate voices barely reached my ears.

Irv
Well, glad that's over!
Roy
Did you like it?
Irv
Sort of, but why did you put a poem about rain here?
Roy
I told you! I have no plan for this book, so anything I put down, I've given no thought.
Irv
You mean it came off the top of your head?
Roy
No! It came off the *bottom* of my head!
Irv
You don't have to get snooty.
Roy
I don't know where the poem came from. No one who calls himself an artist does. They just try it out and see if it works. If it doesn't work they throw it away. Of course some artists keep their work even if it doesn't make any sense, much like I might have done. I may be one of those. Don't hang me, man! I'm still alive and don't plan to kill myself - at least not yet.
Irv
Why did you write Strong Wind and Rain?
Roy
Well, you see I've known wind and rain all my life and the two have been here since the dawn of time. They are what you might call number one and two of the earth's basic elements: *Wet and dry.* Though I never tire of them, they can be vicious and deadly at times. They are more

often nurturing to our planet, the wind scattering seeds to fertile ground with welcome water to enhance planetary growth and to quell the thirst of all that's living. So beneficial are they, I suppose humans could worship them as Gods. But those reasons are intellectual. Rain reminds me of my beloved midwestern childhood living in a small house nestled among cornfields. This was where, as a six-year-old, I slept with my head propped on the windowsill listening to the wind, hearing raindrops hit our thin roof and mild thunder with flashes of light and feeling fine droplets landing on my face.

Irv
OK! That's enough. I get the picture. What other piece of genius have you got for us?

Roy
No more wind and rain?

Irv
I'm filled to here with it!
(Irv hits his neck with the side of his palm.)

Roy
Guess what? I slept through the night and it's the following day. I had a dream!

Irv
Oh no! Don't tell me about it.

Nighttime – Dream #1

I dreamed of a large round metal pan, similar to that for holding pizza, only larger. I later assumed the pan was a symbol of self, or the unknowable location of my personal awareness. Spread evenly over the top of the pan were crumbly white objects similar to popped kernels of corn spaced evenly and close together in a single layer. Each flake represented an essential part of my life including every thought, feeling, hope and dream throughout my entire life, through birth, childhood, adolescence, adult life, marriage, death of my two wives and birth of my three daughters, retirement and old age. This round metal pan was a symbol of *my self* upon which was distributed everything that happened to *"self"* during the vast extension of *my life*.

One flake would represent the singular positive feeling about the first sprinklings of rain after a long drought, another the panicky feelings of death by drowning, the third, the ecstasy of falling in love, the fourth, the joy of accomplishment of a task, etc. Each flake would represent one experience in my long life and you might say was an answer to what I'd been looking for in my later life, a sense of belonging in the present world in which I find myself.

Irv
Well, let's hear it for old Roy! Can we go back to where we were? That is, what's next?
Roy
A word about poetic form.
Irv
What's poetic form?

Roy
Most poems are written in the form of short letters written to the poet himself or herself. They are written up and down in short paragraphs rather than sidewise, line after line, on a flat page of paper. They are expressions putting intimate thoughts and feelings into a manner easily read and remembered, but with so much feeling and brilliance they'll be distinctly understood on a deeper, more feeling level.
Irv
I don't need to know that much.
Roy
I knew you didn't. I'll explain the poem later, if I write one, that will be a poem mostly to myself.
Irv
Do you have anything else for us today?
Roy
No! Yes! I slept last night and had a dream.
Irv
Another dream? Not again?

Nighttime – Dream #2

At about 6:00 AM I had a dream. I was sitting on a handmade cardboard chair at twilight on the beach of a dark ocean. The chair and I were in front of a carelessly built wooden table with three rather undistinguished looking people sitting with me. The chairs, table, people and me were alone at the edge of a dark ocean swallowed in the distance by thick black sky. Inch-deep crystal-clear ocean water rippled over washed sand toward shore running under the table and soaking the bottoms of table legs and the vulnerable bottom of my cardboard chair. The bottom of the cardboard chair was also in the process of disintegration. Surprisingly, the water retreated while returning to the ocean. Within a short period of time our miniscule twilight meeting dissolved in thin air. Half awake and still pondering, I worried about the dream and immediately thought of looking in Wikipedia for Malibu's high and low tides.

Irv
Wow that's exciting! Looking for Malibu's high and low tides. That should be written as a poem. What's next on your list?
Roy
I'm not done yet. There's an interpretation I want to make.
Irv
Oh no! Can't we get on to the more important parts of whatever you have to say?
Roy
There aren't any important parts, just silly things passing through my brain minute-by-minute, hour-by-hour, day-by-day throughout what seems like an eternity!

Irv
OK! Go ahead! I'm stuck with it.
Roy
Using reason, because nature has endowed humans with reason as one of the miracles of our existence, perhaps even more than our imaginative abilities, I will be interpreting the dream. *One* – The night sky, being dark and black, suggests unknown quantities of everything in a cosmic time scale like life and death. *Two* – Sand disappears into the black unknown suggesting our existence moving into the black, mysterious unknown. *Three* – Rippling water undermining my chair *(life)* moves relentlessly away from under the chair and back into the dark unknown, evidently showing me today's not quite the time for death. *Four* – The homemade cardboard chair is weak and vulnerable to decay. *Five* – The tides speak of the world's relentless reactions to the changing of time. It means time's relentless and eventually I will die!
Irv
So, what does that have to do with anything?
Roy
Any fool can see it! I see it! My life exists in the blackness of an unknowable context, confirmed by movable sand, an example of time moving arbitrarily into and out of existence. I sit irrevocably connected to a vulnerable chair susceptible to inevitable decay *(the end of life)*, with water attempting to wear away any protection I might have against death. In time the water recedes, meaning it's not yet my time to die. The tides symbolizing how fast the water rises and falls is a clue as to how much time to live I have left.
Irv
That's kind of depressing. Do you feel better now?

Roy
No! I'm an old man. Good things are coming to an end. How do you expect me to feel?
Irv
Well, fuck you!
Roy
Fuck you, too!
Irv
You want to settle this in the alley?
Roy
You mean to decide who's smarter?
Irv
I'll punch you in the nose and show you who is smarter!
Roy
Yeah! You and who else? OK! OK! You win. I've got another essay. It's entitled *No Life After Death,* you want to hear it?
Irv
Yeah! I guess so. I'm sorry I said "go fuck yourself."
Roy
Forget it!

No Life After Death

In thinking of heaven, everyone seems to have left out animals such as lions and tigers and bears. And then considering afterlife it seems unreasonable that with no bodies or any senses to experience a burger and fries with a Diet Coke, the joys of life and so on, we're to experience pleasure forever under conditions totally unknown to any of those persons alive, awake and aware.

Yet, one of the miracles of human life is the ability to *reason. (If this happens, usually that happens.)* That is, being able to count on basic principles of the cosmos, forever available, necessary and responsible for how they behave, and perfectly trustworthy, particularly in science. Up is never down, in is never out, do is never don't.

Inertia is always reliable. The Sun, Moon, Earth and stars revolving for billions of miles for billions of years, but timed to the second. Love is always in relationship to hate. The Universe expands at a measurable rate. Everything is the opposite of nothing. On Earth, there is only the thickness of a couple of miles of breathable air. Water is water, air is air, rock is rock, etc. Why not one more pair of opposites like life is the opposite of death? Now living things are here and now they're not!

On near-death experiences in Bruce Greyson's book, *After,* when it came to the choice of participants returning to normal life or submitting to death with no mention of returning to life, 80% were tempted to die, because in dying they'd experienced an impossible-to-describe feeling of warmth, love and universal connection so strong it couldn't truthfully be otherwise understood. Greyson's research showed a verified member of the human species with a strong incentive to die - without the so-called expectation of life after death.

This new theory is supposedly an indication of the human condition just before they die, though in actuality most of Greyson's participants didn't die but returned to life. They didn't die like the unfortunate death of animals on the highway called road kill. Besides humans being given our present miracle of remembering the past and planning the future, we also have been given the miracle of music, speech, words, remembering, the opposing thumb and writing books, music, poetry as well as general ingenuity, figuring things out, ideas and invention.

It might be when the time is right, and life is over and it's the proper time to go, that all types of animals would slip into death and sleep through eternity. When living beings have outgrown their natural time, they'd fall into a silent sleep, as the universe continues its merry journey to the end of time, whenever that might be. The bodies of the formerly dead remain as part of the universe eventually contributing as part of the base and fundamentals of ongoing life. To me, it seems more reasonable than living forever after death while not accepting the obvious, the blatant and pre-verified facts. Who else has this theory?

Irv
Are you trying to make this some kind of intellectual book by thinking things out, or whatever?
Roy
No, I'm illustrating how a popular view of heaven might be understood in a more reasonable way. Those who haven't thought much about heaven, or those who have given heaven lots of thought don't seem to have a reasonable alternative to heaven. Their belief could be

for a *preference* for heaven rather than a dislike of no heaven. As in yes or no, or in or out, or up or down, I'm asking the question, is there a heaven, yes or no? The real answer isn't maybe. Or if it's *"maybe,"* my new alternative to maybe for heaven is still no, despite there being a strong preference for the existence of heaven.

Irv
Why do you always give life and death this much thought?

Roy
Because there's an old lesson I've learned called *"Think before you do."* I'd like to add, *"decisions are best when considering the whole."* If I don't consider the whole, what I don't know will work against me in the end. We must put the end result in context as part of the whole. It is my thought, too much effort goes into life forever!

Another scientific theory is that after all the stars in the sky implode into one black hole, unthinkable time evaporates the black hole until the black hole is gone. As the not yet accepted book says, all matter has disappeared by evaporating into nowhere! Will our life after death still be here if the Universe no longer exists? When the sun swallows up the earth in 4½ billion years, does it swallow up heaven? Can nothing, which will be here in 4½ billion years, receive or transmit information? Reason tells me no! Irv! Irv! Irv! Wake up! Wake up!

Irv
Huh? What? What's goin' on?

Roy
You fell asleep.

Irv
No! I heard ya! I heard ya!

Roy
Yeah! What did I say?

Irv
You mumbled something about Think before you do, or . . . Stink before you do. Or do before you stink. Somethin' like that.

Roy
You're the perfect student. I'm sure you're rested

Irv
You got somethin' else?

Roy
Yes! As a matter of fact, I do. It's a question involving humanity. In fact the question involves the rest of the living world.

Irv
Sounds fairly important! What's the question?

Roy
Is there water, and why?

Irv
Of course there is. I could have told you that!

Roy
I don't think my answer is as simple as that.

Irv
Lay it on me. I'll have comments.

Roy
I'm sure you will.

Why is There Water?

Why is there water?
To drink and to swim
To water the bushes
And follow your whim.
Why is there air?

      To huff and to puff
      And blow up balloons
      And enjoy all the stuff.

Why is there Earth?
To dig in the ground
Grow daisies and flowers
And roll all around.
Why are there graves?

      To make big holes
      And bury the dead
      While sharing with moles.

Will you go quickly?
      Not too soon.
      I'll never be ready.
      It's half past noon.

Are you through with questions?
      Going out the door?
      Give me a moment.
      Just one more.
Is there life after death?

      As I understand it,
      yes and it's no.
      An unresolved gamut.

What's it like there?
The silence is massive

With love all around,
Quiet and passive.

But if there's no heaven,
Where will you go?

To sleep forever.
Go home to the Earth.

It's the mother we came from,
The one that gave birth.

Irv
Do you like that poem?
Roy
No. Not really.
Mostly no!
I have nothing to give
but mediocrity!
It's got to be go!
Irv
The poem is not just about water, but questions and answers on air, Earth, graves, heaven and life after death.
Roy
At least it's about something. You can't write about nothing, but now that I think about it I *have* written about nothing.
Irv
Did you like writing about nothing?
Roy
Not much there! Let's change the subject! Again at twilight, I dreamed I was walking on top of a flat,

two-story rooftop. *(Most of my dreams are in twilight. I can't help it. Don't hang me! You're not the boss of me. It's a short dream called Nighttime – Dream #3)*

Irv
Go on.

Nighttime – Dream #3

On top of a ten-story building, there's a middle-aged lady standing near the edge of the roof, when suddenly she jumps off. I see her stiff, dark-clothed body poised and vertical in the air momentarily before she plummets to the ground. I rush to the edge of the roof and look down and see her sprawled body lying face down on the sidewalk, obviously dead on impact. I awake!

Irv
I'm glad I'm not you. What's that all about?
Roy
The dream doesn't seem like a rude awakening, but more like a rude a-deadening. Striking in its symbolism, disturbing in its graphic representation, disquieting in its essence. I don't yet know what it symbolizes. Perhaps it represents unconscious feelings of my own death.
Irv
Let's not dwell on it.
Roy
Get ready for the next colossal poem about time. How long does it take to get from one piece of matter to another? Depends on how fast you're traveling. Sometimes an hour 'til lunch seems forever.
Irv
I can't wait!

Clock Ticking Away

I see a clock ticking away.
Because it's electric
It's not really ticking,
but rolling.

    The hands glide ever so
    slightly I don't see them
    moving. As time goes by

they make their lazy way
around and around,
always left to right,
never right to left,

    on a tireless journey
    to nowhere,
    minute by minute,
    hour by hour,
    day by day,
    year by year
    throughout eternity,
    then an hour more.

Humans count time by
how long it takes to get
from one piece of matter
to another piece of matter.

    No matter, no time.
    If no humans exist,
    no time exists.
    Like Do, without Don't
    Like Yes without No
    Like On without Off

If I never heard of it,
it doesn't exist.
But, I exist,
how or why,
birth to death,
or by what means,
no one knows, but if
I exist, time exists.

So, how long it takes
getting from one matter
to another matter, is
only defined by me
and the clocks.

Irv
That's pretty good. Any dreams or anything?
Roy
Not today.
Irv
Good! You care about clocks or anything?
Roy
I've got one I care about called anthropomorphism!
Irv
I'm not familiar with that word.
Roy
I didn't expect you to be. Anthropomorphism means the attribution of human characteristics to God, animals or an object. The essay is called *Anthropomorphism and the Serious Architect*. It's where I ask the elements of architecture how they feel about their inclusion, an essential necessity for a piece of art.
Irv
Does the house talk back?
Roy
It does in surprising ways. Let's talk about it.

Anthropomorphism the Serious Architect

Anthropomorphism in this essay means *"attributing human qualities to anything not human." (In this case, buildings.)*

Serious Architect means one who has been educated in the fundamentals of living in certain places and someone building homes for those suitably wealthy. I am *not* discussing the average mass-produced house done at a minimum *(or maximum)* cost for needs and profit from a future buying community.

The people responsible for bringing into the world whatever unique house is created are the owners, architects and contractor. But, the one with the greatest education and the most expertise is the architect. He should be the most responsible.

During the architect's creative process, the program, or what the house has to do, is the major question he must answer.

Part of the program is the site, which must be listened to because, though it is without words, it speaks loud and clear. It faces south or doesn't, has a prevailing wind or doesn't, has a view or doesn't, and many other qualities that it may or may not possess, all of which have to be addressed, solved and accounted for.

Not cooperating with the site invites a fight. Flowing with the site is generally right. The owner may have to give up a quality he thought he already possessed. Going with the flow and with the site means the building will build easier with a natural look as if it grew there.

This is a good thing.

Irv
That was really good news. I am glad to know that. Now I wish I had the money to build a house, but don't expect I ever will.
Roy
Don't lose hope. Perhaps a bag of money will fall out of the sky, Then, all your worries will be over.
Irv
I sure am going to hope for that. Do you hope for that?
Roy
No! Not especially. Just now I have to write this book, Now and then I just need to blow my horn. As my Dad used to say, I ain't got nuthin' to do anyway. Space-time is a mathematical model that joins space and time into a single idea called a continuum, but you probably wouldn't want to know more about that.
Irv
No, I'd rather have a hamburger.
Roy
I'm not sure I could tell you more about that myself. I've read a bunch of books on that subject and I still don't know what they're talking about.
Irv
Yeah! Me too! I'd say forget it. Have you got a Snicker's bar up your sleeve?
Roy
Let me look. No! Here's an idea called,
When I Was a Boy.

When I Was a Boy

When I was a boy and six years old, it had been raining outside in the back of our house; big droplets splashed in my hair and forehead and covered my face with smaller droplets. They were the ones I could lick off and still be smiling. Even though I'm old, I remember with joy when I was happy about all that existed - mainly my own existence and the presence and wonder of rain.

Sometimes, I'd like to be a child again because rain brought peace, but at this time in my life, that's impossible. So here I sit, old and remembering days of the past, wishing I were there. Age has its bad moments and yet I'm glad to be alive even considering personal elderly circumstances.

So what is an old person going to do with his life considering the fact that he remembers the past and thinks about not having a very long future?

There seems no alternative, but I suppose it has to do with what is in front of me. The past is gone so I can't do anything there. And so you might ask now what shall I do? Writing and art are the only things that come to mind. Maybe I should be a good guy to keep my friends, so I'll devote myself to that, too!

Irv
That was really short. If you'd left that out, the book wouldn't have lost a thing. That is, assuming the book had any grain of thought to start with.
Roy
You didn't like the story?
Irv
The story of your childhood?

Roy
It was more of a question about what an old person is going to do with his life now most of it's gone.
Irv
Why not ask your readers?
Roy
You're right! I should delete those paragraphs. Who cares what I was like when I was a boy, or how an elderly person ends his life? Nobody gives a damn! Except for me, of course.
Irv
Well, now, don't go too far. After all, how are your readers going to know who you really are if you're not perfectly candid with them? You're boring sometimes, but I'd say keep it in. You can always delete it later.
Roy
You're right. I can always delete it later. Are you ready for a poem about my former business?
Irv
No! But I don't think that answer will stop you.
Roy
Here's a poem from several years ago about standard conditions during times of brush fire in my former Malibu architectural practice. I think you're going to remember and thank me for the occasional Blank Statement of *God's Awful Truth* for the rest of your life.

God's Awful Truth

If I'd lost everything and
didn't have something to do
to get my teeth into and feel
like I was solving problems,
I'd be in bad shape.

        Such is not the case.
        I'm working hard and can see
        real progress in our financial
        situation as well as some nice
        architectural stuff coming out.

I've got some great clients
who are really concerned
about doing good building.

        Fortunately, Malibu is
        an affluent area, and after
        the fire, wealthy people
        wanted their houses back.

Also there is talk of the
government making 3%
loans available.
Isn't that la, la?

        If you ever get slow in your
        work, just burn down
        your neighborhood
        and set up business on
        the Coast Highway.
        That's the way to do it.

Plans done cheap! I really
liked that bit in the Sears catalog,
$200.00 for a set of plans ... *Free!*

I think I'll send away for
free plans for our new house.

Irv
That poem's kind of ironic?
Roy
You think so? What's ironic mean?
Irv
*"Happening in the opposite way to that which is expected
and typically causing wry amusement because of this."*
Roy
Hey! That sounds smart! I didn't know you were
intelligent!
Irv
I copied the definition of ironic from the Internet.
Roy
I see that now! Ironic doesn't sound too bad. Would you
like to read *Topsy-Turvy Design?*
Irv
If I have to, I will.

Topsy-Turvy Design

A picture of topsy-turvy design
set my imagination free to roam.
Where does *topsy-turvy* take me?

> Out to sea? No!
> To Hell and back? No!
> Visiting a foreign
> city in my dreams? Yes!

I dreamed I was visiting
Bulgaria on the west coast of the
Black Sea. Dressed in conventional
day clothes, my wife and I
ascended wide stone stairs
leading to a monumental building.

> Hundreds of important people
> were invited to the Prime Minister's
> birthday party, and as we climbed
> I was shocked to notice with each
> of my steps up the stairs our
> clothes made a step backwards.

By the time we reached a broad
landing and wide swinging doors,
our clothes looked like those
of the *Roaring Twenties*.

> My wife suddenly had bobbed
> hair, a slim flapper hat, long skirt,
> and flesh-colored stockings.
> I discovered myself with a
> black tuxedo and shiny black
> shoes and wearing a *Derby* hat.

By the time we reached the large,
ornate room, all the women
wore 18th century hoop skirts,
petticoats and corsets to support
their breasts and I found myself
with a stiff collar, high-wasted
trousers, gray vest and both of us
irrevocably trapped in another age.

Roy
What did you think of that idea?
Irv
I think at times you're kind of reaching for it, aren't you, Roy?! Hey! Here comes Nancy! How'd you get here, Nancy?
Nancy
I was just walking home from my Russian Society group meeting in Malibu.
Irv
*I'd like you to meet my friend, Roy. Roy, Nancy!
How many are in your Russian Society group?*
Nancy
We have 24 members. I've been with them three years, am president, and my job is inspiring new and old members.
Irv
How you doin' with that?
Nancy
In the past month we've read five books by Shostakovich, Nabokov, Chekhov, Dostoyevsky and Tolstoy.
Irv
No shit! That's a lot of books. You must be really smart.
Nancy
When you read so many books you can't help being smart. I've read thousands of books, so I guess I'm really

smarter than everybody. Ask me something.
Irv
What's the square root of sixteen?
Nancy
Four!
Irv
I think that's right. Is that right, Roy?
Roy
I'm not a mathematician. It could be right.
Nancy
I've got to run along. Schrodingy, Boogar & Matchmouth are giving a lecture!
Irv
You wouldn't want to miss that.
See you next time, Nancy! Whatcha' got next, Roy?
Roy
Nancy is a beautiful and interesting young woman. How did you come to know her?
Irv
In grammar school, we were together in the tiddlywink competitions. I always won!
Roy
I'd like to see her again.
Irv
I'm sure you will.
Roy
I've dug up another brilliant, imaginative piece for you. It's called, *Life After Death*.
Irv
That's sounds really gloomy. It's hard to beat the last one about getting up in the modern age and traveling back in time only to be trapped in the 18th century. Come to think of it, that wasn't so good either.

Life After Death

My heart goes, tick, tick,
tick and keeps me alive
so I can do what I do
and be who I am.

I ask my self,
Who am I?

> I am many versions of man
> including a right-brained person
> mostly of feelings
> who tells me
> *what* can make me happy
> and a left-brained person
> who tells me
> *how* to make me happy.

Leading directly to a
very popular question:
Is there life after death?

> Humanity wants to answer yes
> because humanity can't imagine the
> eternal emptiness of non-existence.

Humans have seen death
through wars, illness,
natural disasters and
day to day dying;
by pandemics, old age,
or disruptions happening
through normal imperfections
and varieties

of circumstances
of normal life.

Many living beings have
died as food for animals.
Billions have died in wars,
disease, childbirth and old age.

Is preference for
Life After Death
a truth or just hoped for?

Roy
What do you think of that idea?
Irv
I'm speechless!
Roy
I thought you would be. The place to see miracles is remembering plans for the future. When all that goes away, I speculate there isn't anything to take its place. When you're here, you're here. When you're gone, so is everything.
Irv
No! When I die I will have another consciousness even better than the one I have now. And with the new consciousness, I will also have a new set of feelings that will be beyond my present set of feelings and I will get much more out of life than I have out of the present titanic group of brilliant miracles.
Roy
I see that as a preference. I can't visualize it better than our miraculous and astounding reality.
Irv
That's because you don't have my imagination.

Roy
What do you imagine?
Irv
I don't know, it's just a feeling.
Roy
I know your feeling is true for you. Feeling of what is my question? Forgetting an answer to a question that seems impossible to answer, it's time to deliberate on an easier question described below.

Blazondon or Hick-up High?

Blazondon High had big fast, handsome players with beautiful uniforms in the latest colors with large white numbers and nicknames on the back. They pranced out on the field as if they owned it, which they did, in front of an immense home crowd that yelled and screamed and waved their arms. They had three backup teams sitting in perfect organization on end-to-end benches. Their twelve gorgeous, short-skirted pompom cheerleaders cartwheeled and made a tower with the queen cheerleader on the top, who yelled and cheered for the fans, and they had an award-winning coach with thick, white, close-cropped hair who cursed the competition and hugged his players.

Hick-up High School had eleven regulars with seven backup players sitting this way and that on throwaway picnic benches and a coach who couldn't make the game because he had to drive his wife to work, but sent an alcoholic assistant who sat on the bench with his head in his hands due to an overhang. Their short quarterback had a long nose with narrow eyes and bad throwing arm, and limped onto the field with a bad knee among boos from his own fans who were only a few. The players were light, short, fat and skinny in mud-colored uniforms with faded numbers still tangy-smelling, since they hadn't been washed in the last three games in which they were embarrassingly defeated again and again and again by enormous scores. They strolled on the field arguing and hitting each other on the helmet or arm, while five poorly dressed, overweight cheerleaders, wearing too much lipstick, gave half-hearted cheers like they needed to be someplace else.

Blazondon High beats ***Hick-up High*** by a score of ***125 to zip*** and all the winners, while running off the field, were healthy and laughing. They had to shower before driving in their Jags and Beamers to the big celebration dinner given in their honor where they'd be served filet mignon and country club dancing with gorgeous coeds after.

Hick-up High players went directly to the hospital and some to the emergency ward. A few relatives traveled in Pintos and Falcons to mourn the health of their players, pay their hospital bills and incidentally complain about the outcome of the game.

For which team would you like to play, **Blazondon High School or Hick-up High School?**

Team _____

Signature here_____

You're selected.

Irv
I used to play for Hick-Up High! I signed up!
Roy
You're kidding. I thought I invented Hick-Up High.
Irv
No! No! I played first-string guard for Hick-Up High. There weren't enough players to have a second string. I played every game. I was rough, tough and didn't take ding-dong for an answer. Coach was a drunk. We were bad in practice. We forgot plays and really stunk!
Roy
That's how I expected Hick-Up High School's team would be. Though it was a work of my imagination,

I couldn't have called it more correctly. Did you like playing for Hick-up High?
Irv
It was OK except for the drunken coach, losses and injuries. Oh yeah! There were also unattractive uniforms and ragged cheerleaders.
Roy
Shall we change the subject? How about a poem called *Early in the Afternoon?*
Irv
Yeah! I guess so. If I have to, I will!

Early in the Afternoon

Taking a nap early in the
afternoon I awoke face
down on my stomach
cemented to the couch
with scrambled memories
of a dream the night before.

    I was standing stiff, straight
    when I noticed my clutched
    hands around a colored object
    the size of a football.
    It was the warmest
    combination of red and
    orange and very smooth.

I held it against my chin
like a bowling ball
ready to throw a strike,
but instead, I felt compelled
to throw the ball far away,
and lofted it high into the air.

    With my eyes,
    I followed its flight
    through the sky
    watching it get
    smaller and smaller
    until it dropped to the
    ground and disappeared.

I visualized it
hitting the ground
with a severe impact
and partially breaking

apart, like a tomato
accidentally dropped on
the floor next to the counter.

I assumed seeds of
information were released
through cracks in the balls
surface, thereto spreading
information in philosophy,
psychology, health and humor
to the public at large.

I lay fifteen minutes, or so,
in my shadow life,
or dreamlike nature.
analyzing the picture.

Irv
Well, Whoop-de-Doooo!
Roy
That's your comment after me struggling to bring something of reality out of thin air? Whoop-de-Doooo?! And that's it? I'm discouraged with you as a friend! You, who are supposed to be seeing the better part of humanity and acting as a sounding board for all that's good and right in the world and all you can come up with is *"Whoop-de-Dooooo!?"*, as if Armand Duplantis, the world champion in the pole vault who holds the world's record of 20'-2-3/4" was just a scam?
Irv
I'm not sure your poem holds the world's record for poetry.
Roy
Well, fuck you!

Irv
Fuck you, too!
Roy
I gave it my best shot!
Irv
Anything else up your sleeve?
Roy
I had another dream!
Irv
Is this a dream journal?
Roy
I'm glad I have dreams. Only alive people have dreams. Dead people have no dreams.
Irv
So, a dream is proof you're alive.
Roy
Exactly! And uses up book space.
Irv
We can't let that escape, can we?
Roy
In old age, I seem to sleep too long. It's as though I had narcolepsy! Narcolepsy is sleeping too much usually when there's nothing else to do anyway. Last night I slept 10 hours, and after breakfast felt the need for more rest, and laid my gentle head down on a gentle pillow on my gentle couch in my gentle living room under the gentle window and was soon blasting off unconscious hours well into a brand new day. But as time dallied its determined way, I finished resting and was compelled to open my eyes. What should I find staring me in the face?
Irv
Oh no! Another dream!!!

Nighttime - Dream #4

It began with an early day trip to the boatyard on the Malibu seashore, except in reality there is no boatyard on the Malibu seashore, and in the dream it could have been any boatyard on the seashore any morning of the bright blue sea in the grasp of a cloud-driven sky. I went past a tangle of boats where there was a long, 10-inch wide concrete slab on edge projecting above the ocean's surface about 4 or 5 feet, evidently a breakwater extending a great distance out to sea before coming to an abrupt stop. The slab on edge driving deep into the water was quickly lost in the watery depths. Being an adventurous middle-aged man in the dream, I decided to walk out to sea on top of the 10-inch wide concrete slab's edge a thousand or so yards to the end of the breakwater.

I continued along the 10-inch wide concrete top as the soft rolling rhythms of the swells four or five feet below made their way shoreward. When the breakwater stopped and disappeared below into the ocean, I sat down straddling the concrete a foot from the end. I enjoyed myself and felt free as the wind and part of something larger than myself. I was encouraged to take my time and think my thoughts, but a gentle breeze from the shoreline drifted past representing the possibility of an approaching storm. This would not be good.

I made my way back along the 10-inch wide concrete top to where I thought I'd got on, though in the first place I had no recollection of ever mounting the top of the concrete breakwater at all. *(It's a dream, so why should I?)* But there was an obscure entrance to a boat anchored closer to shore, and if I made a little jump I could be on it and ask directions from anyone aboard. I did, and made my way through the cabin door, and found about six people inside the cabin with lights totally out. A window at the rear made a strong glare so that my eyes could not pick up the appearance of any faces. When I introduced myself, people seemed to welcome me and one person in the back said he knew me, though I could not see who he was.

Since the group did not say anything or answer my questions, nothing transpired during my short visit. I exited to the small rear deck from which I'd entered, but the top of the 10-inch wide breakwater would demand a jump far too long for me to risk. I returned to the cabin and could see a little better. There were three fully clothed, middle-aged men kissing three fully clothed, middle-aged women and I woke up.

Irv
What am I going to do with you? Why is there no reasonable end? Why do we have to go through dreams?
Roy
I just thought it would bring one more story to life's surface to enlighten and enrich the total of mortal experiences and expanding, if ever so little, total human knowledge, if anybody else ever read this book
Irv
Hooray for you!
Roy
Haven't you ever heard the expression, *"Do what you can to brighten life's little corner"*?
Irv
You mean that dream brightened my corner?
Roy
Perhaps made it a little brighter. I ask myself what I could do to brighten my little corner of life? The answer is *analyzing it!* If traveling outward on the long 10-inch wide breakwater thrusting four or five feet out of water,

provokes a unique adventure and if I go to the end, there's the risk of falling in the ocean and drowning. So the dream is not only exciting, but is also risky. So I ask myself in real life, what could be the comparable experience I'm taking involving excitement and risk? I'm candid answering reality has forced me to continue life's journey into old age, *(the concrete water-wall)* and when I get to the end, a storm might blow me off to my death. *(The danger of drowning)* Anything new I discover is, as it is to everybody, new to me. The difference is I've already seen 94 years of life and those who've died in less time have not seen as many years. Therefore, if I've not forgotten my past, while risking the end, I continue to gain knowledge about the future. Isn't that a gas? I hereby make the statement: Nothing will not experience anything?

Irv
Is that brightening your little corner?

Roy
Yes! It brightens my personal little corner and the corners of those with whom I communicate. But there is the end of the dream to consider. I'm not able to communicate with six persons in the room. I can't see them and they are not part of my life. To me, they've died! I don't know them and they don't know me. This is a strong part of the dream. At death, I'm still in the dark as to what's going to happen and forced to wait and see. Normally, the aged have joined those who've already died and tend to be at least partially forgotten by those still living and actively pursuing their own lives.

Irv
Bummer!

Roy
To summarize, there are two meanings to the dream: *One* is that living to an old age is forcing me to continue life's positive adventures while at the risk of physical and

mental deterioration. *Two* is that, while feeling love and erotic overtones, I continue benefitting from relationships with friends and offspring.
Irv
Let's hear it for old Roy!
Roy
Shall we get on with it? Oh look, here comes Nancy. Hiya! Nancy! What brings you to this neck-o-da woods, or delivers fuel to us old battleships drifting haphazardly on life's dangerous seas, if you'll pardon my exuberant, mundane and stupid expression?
Nancy
Hiya, Roy! I'm just coming back from our Gilbert and Sullivan rehearsal, wherein next Saturday I'll be playing the part of Bunthorne's Bride, the female lead, in Gilbert and Sullivan's operetta, *Patience.*
Irv
Hiya, Nancy. Why don't you give us a little solo rendition.
Nancy
OK! How about a humorous little number from *Patience?* *(In a beautiful soprano voice, she sings the following song from* Patience *usually sung by a male.)*

If you're anxious for to shine
in the high aesthetic line
as a man of culture, rare?

You must get up all the germs
of transcendental terms
and plant them everywhere.

You must lie upon the daisies
and count in novel phrases
of your complicated state of mind.

*The meaning doesn't matter
if it's only idle chatter
of a transcendental kind.*

And ev'ry one will say,
as you walk your mystic way,
*"If this young man expresses himself
in terms too deep for me, why what
a very singularly deep young man
this deep young man must be!"*

Irv
Bravo! Bravo! That was outstanding! Did you like it, Roy?
Roy
That was superb, Nancy! You wanna' stay around, kick dirt and talk?
Nancy
No! I gotta' be off. Doreen is waiting for me. She sings alto in our group and also takes a part with us in our play-reading group. We're just finishing an autobiographical masterpiece by Anna Ahmatova-bunky, one of the few Russian women writers. She was born in 1889 and died in 1966 at the age of 77. Isn't that a squeaky hinge? Must be off! Ta-ta!
Irv
Ta-ta! I mean, goodbye! Take it easy! See you soon! Don't be mad! I'm in love with you!
Roy
I got a good one for ya' Irv.
Irv
Yeah? What's that?
Roy
I Lay There Pondering. You'll see!

I Lay There Pondering

It was too much.
I lay there pondering.
In fact it was mind-boggling!
Harold had dozed off.

    In the pitch dark a light
    flashed on, moved a short
    distance, then flashed off.

    Then another light flashed on,
    circled about, then went out.

    I thought to myself, *"Fireflies!"*
    Quickly, another flash,
    Zig-zagged, then off.

Then another and another
until the sky around, indeed,
the whole marshy reeds
were filled with hundreds
of fireflies, some high, some
low, some floating on still air,
some blown softly by the breeze,
all quiet, soft, gentle, self-lighting
their journeys. It was comforting
to me that this violent planet
could have fireflies.

    I was reminded of pre-
    adolescent vacations
    in upstate New York.

Presently a stronger breeze
whistled in from across the sea

and fluttered the tops of reeds,
and in the quiet I could hear the
movement of their palm-like
tops. And then I caught the
fragrance of Jasmine floating
on the wind as if from a field
of flowers that had gently
seeped into the reeds.

As the speed of wind increased
and blew with a little more force,
it brought the sound of ocean waves
crashing softly on the sand and I
thought of tomorrow's adventures.

Then, as the fireflies were blown away,
the breeze took the aroma of Jasmine,
and soon the wind and I drifted off.

Irv
You and the wind drifted off? I think you and your mind drifted off! People don't drift off on the wind; they're too heavy. What if I said, the freight train drifted off in the wind. They'd lock me up!
Roy
The phrase, *the wind and I drifted off* illustrates the use of a metaphor. Do you know what a metaphor is, Irv?
Irv
No!
Roy
I thought not. A metaphor is describing one thing by reference to another, such as *"an early bird catches the worm"* means one who gets up early and makes progress quicker than one who doesn't.

Irv
So, in other words, being smart takes more work.
Roy
If you like what you're doing it's not work.
Irv
I'm exhausted! Oh boy! Here comes Nancy. She's got someone with her. Hiya! Nancy! Who ya got witcha?
Nancy
Hiya, Irv! Hiya, Roy! This is Eloise, who is the American Balance Beam Gymnast Champion. Next week we're flying to Norway and competing in the Norwegian-American Balance Beam championship.
Roy
Hiya, Nancy and Eloise! Welcome to our home grounds, wherever that is. Nancy, do you perform gymnastics for the American balance beam team, too?
Nancy
As a matter of fact, yes I do! Besides being president of the American-Russian Book Club and having just sung the part of Bunthorne's Bride in last week's countrywide production of Gilbert and Sullivan's musical play, *Patience*, I was also the American champion balance beam performer in last year's American-Norwegian competitions. I will probably win this year's competition as well.
Irv
Hi ya! Eloise, what's your special trick to wow the spectators in the world-renowned balance bar - - - I mean, balance beam competitions?
Eloise
Well, as two of this world's greatest balance beam gymnasts living today, Nancy, and me, here, both have worked all year learning the most difficult *front-running back one-and-one-half somersaults with two-and-a-half twists* without landing on the beam crotch-first and splitting ourselves in two.

(Writer's clarification: There is no dive in the Olympics or anywhere called the front running back 1½ somersault with 2½ twists. This dive is impossible and included here only for mildly humorous purposes. If it were a serious dive, the contestant would begin by standing erect at the beginning of the board, hair combed and looking the perfect human specimen. He or she would then take two steps forward, lifting one knee high in the air before dropping to bounce the board and shooting him or her straight into the air, arms and hands symmetrical, pointing skyward, while twisting a one-half turn prior to again landing on the board and bouncing once again into one-and-a-half somersaults with two-and-a-half twists. In competitive diving, no one bounces the board twice on a single dive. Ha! Ha! Ha! I think!)

Irv
How do you practice that?
Eloise
We've invented a sort of bulletproof-vest like thing that slips under our trunks in case upon occasion we make some life shattering mistake.
Irv
That's very inventive of you, don't you think, Roy? Why couldn't I have thought of that?
Roy
Because you know nothing of gymnastics or the balance bar - - - I mean balance beam?
Irv
You've got me there!
Nancy
Eloise is known as *The Whirling Balance Ball of Beams*, rarely missing the death-defying trick, except once in Idaho. Remember that, Eloise?
Eloise
How could I forget?

Irv
That's why Nancy and Eloise are world-renowned and the absolute shoo-ins for winning Norway's top ticket.
Nancy
I'd bet on myself! We're off to do better things! *(Both said in unison.)* Goodbye, Roy, goodbye, Harve!
Irv
That's Irv!
Eloise
Sorry! Goodbye, Irv!
Irv
Whatcha got next, Roy?
Roy
Something a little different, Irv. It's a story beginning on another planet that's visited by a spaceship with a bunch of adventures and introducing someone special.
Irv
Is it real?
Roy
It's as real as you might expect in a book like this.

Another American

Over the next minute or so,
the image of the black dot
became intelligible and the
hum more pronounced
until it slowed and with

> clarity and control, floated
> fifty-feet above the center of the
> landing area. The craft paid no
> attention to gravity as it hovered
> high and stationary in the air.

With smooth sides the aircraft
was circular and black about
thirty-feet in diameter being
heftier or thicker in the middle.

> It had what looked like a glass
> top for observing the cosmos and
> marvels of starry evenings, while
> beneath were four decorative landing
> gears aesthetically intertwined.

With a rev and hum from its underside,
four landing gears emerged with
wheels attached and quietly the
strange craft descended and gently
settled on a grassy platform.

> After a few seconds, the engine's
> drone fell silent and with oiled
> efficiency, a side of the aircraft
> with stairs lowered to the ground
> upon which six foreigners descended

wearing strange green caps.
Among them my spirits rose at
the sight of a medium-sized
American gentleman also arriving,
albeit another lapse in this strange,
impossible terrain. I walked

    briskly forward while the
    gentleman approached with
    great enthusiasm. We extended
    our arms for a friendly handshake.
    The new stranger said, *"I'm Harold.*
    Glad to meet a fellow American."

Roy
Well! How'd you like that one?
Irv
I wouldn't a-thrown it against the wall!
Roy
That's nice of you to say and exactly the comment I'd expect from a guy like you.
Irv
I'm nobody's ding-dong! Where'd you come up with that idea?
Roy
Writing a novel was coming nicely, but I couldn't think of an ending.
Irv
How'd it start?
Roy
A marriageable-aged male protagonist closed his eyes, sneezed, and found himself on another planet in weird surroundings.
Irv
Pro – tag a – a - nist? Wha? Yes! Yes! Go on!

Roy
In the story, there's lots of water, too-tall trees, two suns, no moon, heavy tides, lots of rain, magic flying machines, a government of smart little chimpanzee-like Doo-dahs running around fighting off dangerous invaders. But that's another story.
Irv
Sounds better than this one.
Roy
Fuck you!
Irv
Fuck you, too!
Roy
You want to settle this in the alley and find out who's smarter?
Irv
No!
Roy
OK! Let's get on with it, then. This book's far from done. Sorry I said *"fuck you!"* The next article is really a little essay that speaks directly to my personal life. It should be in an autobiographical volume instead of here, in the sense that this whole book is really part of a scrambled autobiography. That's why the book might be called *Disparities.* The next essay is called *Dream and Desires.* Brace yourself!

Dream and Desires

About 4:15 AM, with the fan on sweeping motion to lower a too-hot temperature, I was awakened by a disturbing dream. I had a vision of myself opening a flat file drawer, and in the drawer were dried vellum papers, brown and discolored with uneven edges; blank, as if never having been used. In the dream, while thinking and considering my age of 87 years and nine months and having a new architectural job, I was stricken with panic and awoke with the recollected horror still on me. I lay awake for some time trying to put the feeling and reality together. Many things occurred. Here are some of them.

I felt the unconscious mind, *the elephant,* was trying to tell the conscious mind, the *rider,* something the unconscious feared – which could have been one of the reasons I'd been feeling anxious and being in the doldrums; having periods of depression, anxiety and the futile sense of *life* being over.

The dream was reminiscent of reoccurring dreams I have had in later life, of having a disordered office in Malibu in a deteriorating building I was worried about; of it being publicly known that I had not paid rent and my fears the building owner evicting me or demanding rent I was unable to pay.

The feelings I had with my reoccurring dreams feeling compromised as a Malibu architect were that better architects, having no trouble paying the rent, might look on me as an interloper and fad unable to be taken seriously and inferior.

Those dreams led me back to thoughts of my being an architect at all. Being an architect was not something I'd thought of for myself. As an adolescent I had no inclination of what I wanted to do in life. I was thinking along the lines of involvement in art without any special interest in art. I assumed I was artistic because I got a scholarship to the Chicago Art Institute at the end of eighth grade from a very uninspired Lowell Grammar School near Humboldt Park in the City of Chicago, which by the way, I only attended about two or three times out of eight of the Institutes 1½-hour lessons. My high school thoughts were mostly of sports: football, track and swimming. Intellectual studies were an unavoidable effort.

I'm reminded, at the age of 13 when my mother's newspaper man father died, I originated the idea of doing a pencil drawing of a Roman soldier by the use of grid guidelines over a miniature picture of Perseus with sword in hand, holding aloft the severed head of Medusa. Mother and dad and my aunts and uncles were impressed and I thought it was pretty good. *"Was it art?"* If not, my drawing, certainly of the statue, from which the picture had been taken, was excellent. Referring again to the dream, mother advised me to study architecture because there was no money in art, but supposedly there was in architecture, and it required an artistic aptitude that I seemed to have. Also, the high school I attended had a three-year college preparatory course in architecture. Studying art in high school was a non-preparatory course for college. I suspect this had a major impact on my decision, and also I did what seemed to be correct to do, that is, follow the advice my mother had given me. You might say my mother decided my future career for me.

In high school, I liked the blank board and the architectural drawings I could produce. I was good at it. My high school architectural courses helped me skip the first semester of architectural drawing at the University of Illinois.

One of our first design projects at the University of Illinois was to design a house. I had no idea of what a house looked like from an architectural standpoint. What did a floor plan look like? What did a house look like from the inside? How did it look from the outside? I'd lived in houses, but if I were to build one, I didn't really see them as I needed to see them. The building's reality escaped me. I had never been interested in houses. At my young age, houses I lived in were already there, and as a child, I adapted as almost everyone does unconsciously to live inside those existing spaces the best way I could.

Having skipped the first semester of design at the University of Illinois, the second semester program required the class to design a single-family residence. I was mind-boggled! Mother helped with a suggestion. She said when I was 3 or 4 years old, our family lived in a pretty good house with a pretty good floor plan. Perhaps I could use it for the second semester school design. I thought so, too. That certainly took the sting out of having to design one for myself. In a creative field, I could skip the creative part and just copy something somebody else had already designed. I did copy it and got a reasonable grade.

I've always felt the design of my first house did not come from me. I never got enthused about creating a new house. I was never pushed from my gut to bring something new into the world. My first effort was stolen, or might be termed a *crib*. I went along with it because it was easy and allowed me to progress. Mother also seemed to go along with it. She didn't admonish me and say, *"You have to create a new house all by yourself."*

And perhaps it was OK to copy a good house. Perhaps, that would be a good way to learn. Of course, as college continued with tests, sketch problems, spending whole semesters on one building, I eventually had to be creative. Perhaps this is the way people learn to do new things.

This covers my early experiences with architecture. If opening a flat file drawer and considering doing a new building throws me into a panic, where does the panic come from? If dreams about having a rundown, poorly organized office in Malibu and being bothered about not paying rent and *getting away with something* are reoccurring, I guess that's the reason?

It would seem panic was caused by something in the past. What occurs to me is that being an architect, though I might be good at it, was not my idea. But I have to say I didn't have any idea as to what my life's work should be. I went along always taking just the next step, because after a college course in architecture, there was nothing else I knew how to do.

I have a hard time admitting these thoughts, but they have relevance. *"I was someone who took the next step."* I followed the rules. I studied architecture in school and got reasonable grades. When I graduated, I got a job as a draftsman. I got my license quickly before I forgot what I'd learned in school. I went into business myself because that was the next step. When times were hard, I remained in architecture and did nothing to escape architecture, just tried to get more architectural work.

In a sense, I did not think for myself, I let *the next step* pull me through life. Now, at the end of architecture, I have had a career. It turns out it was a good one. I'm proud of the way I conducted my business. Given the sincere love of my family, it was the only way it could have turned out. Limited by my talent, I did the best I could. How better a career could I ask for? So why do I now experience the panic?

Answer

My inner person didn't especially like being an architect. Perhaps I would have preferred being an artist or writer or both. At this time I had made an announcement to my publisher, Helane Freeman, that since I'm no longer a practicing architect, I'd spend my remaining years making books and doing artwork.

Any reoccurring dreams that had to do with continuing to be an architect was reacted to strongly by my *elephant*, the unconscious mind; it didn't want to do that. It panicked! Instead of continuing to practice architecture, I would pursue another line of work for which I was suited, and be an artist and writer. Conclusion: If you truly know what your deepest desires are, pursue them!

Irv
That sure was a lot of reading!
Roy
I hoped I had something to say. What did I say?
Irv
You made it clear that in life, you never wanted to be anything.
Roy
After the dream I asked myself why I had such a depressing and self-loathing view of my life and that it was over! The dream's answer indicated I'd made my decision that to do what I did was a monumental *but technically forgivable* mistake. The dream made me aware that doing what I did made me think I was inadequate in the real world and that I was nothing more than a fad and unable to be taken seriously. The reoccurring dream was powerful enough that I needed to pursue the answer and find out what it meant. In so doing, my memory slowly returned, leading me to know

the series of events I followed to my lifelong architectural profession. What follows is Grammar School Scholarship to Chicago Art Institute, three years of high school architecture, U of I college architecture, license, work as a draftsman and opening my own business and future for a lifetime. With not enough time to correct the problem, the dream was an expression of unaddressed panic of having continued a not-self-chosen lifelong work. Life was over with no correction possible.

Irv
You didn't die or anything. Things could have been worse.
Roy
That's true. Everyone meets life at least halfway. If you lose a leg, haven't you got another? If you lose an eye, you've got another one, haven't you? If you become paraplegic, you're still alive, aren't you? So, I guess if I didn't follow another pattern I might have chosen, at least I didn't die, did I? The answer is no, so I'm trying to feel lucky.
Irv
Is it working?
Roy
Yes and no.
Irv
What're ya gonna do?
Roy
Suck it up!
Irv
Good plan! What's next?
Roy
I'm feeling sad, so I'm gonna' have to write down a final philosophy called, *Suck it up!*

Suck it Up!

One for the two,
two for the three,
three for the four
and get ready to live!
For this is the first day
of the rest of my life
and if I've not got it now,
it's too little too late, so
face the hard facts and,
Suck it Up!

Irv
That was a really bad poetic attempt!
Roy
I never said I was great!
Irv
Here comes Nancy. Maybe she'll bring a little happiness into our lives. Hiya, Nancy! Who ya got witcha?
Nancy
Eloise and Koo Koo Kakootchna! Koo Koo is Lithuania's top balance beam gymnast and her country is attempting to compete against us in the Norwegian-American championship in a three-way between America, Norway and Lithuania.
Irv
No shit!
Nancy
But Norway is fighting Lithuania's entrance because *they-done-wanna-do-it* with three countries. America's takes the attitude, *"Hey! It's your problem!"*
Irv
Let me know how that turns out!

Roy
Hiya, Nancy! You sure are pretty.
Nancy
Hiya, Roy! Yeah, I know I'm pretty. That's what most people say. I'm a champion balance beam gymnast, but also the lead singer of the famous American Gilbert & Sullivan operatic society and president of the American-Russian Book Club reading a bunch of famous Russian writers including Dostoyevsky and Chekov. Aren't I great? We're leaving now!
Irv
Goodbye and nice meeting you Koo Koo – ah – I mean Miss Kakootchna, and Eloise. Oh, yeah! You too, Nancy.
Koo Koo
Goodbye, Oiv!
Irv
That's Irv!
Eloise
Goodbye, Irv and Roy!
Irv
G'bye Eloise! Whatcha' got comin' up, Roy?
Roy
Yeah! This one's dedicated to you.

Mars and Me

Stephen Hawking was telling me
The size of the Universe!
My answer was, "What?"
He said it was really big.
I said *"Huh?"*
He said if you walked from Mars
    To Jupiter, you'd be late for dinner.
My ready response was,
"That far, eh?
We could carry a snack!"
You're missing the point.
"What?"
You don't know the consequences!
"Huh?"
YOU FOOL! The point is distance, not food.
    "Oh!"

    Irv
You're dedicating that to me?
    Roy
If the shoe fits, wear it!
    Irv
I don't think I'm that dumb.
Who's Stephen Hawking, anyway?
    Roy
That question just proved my point.
    Irv
Haven't we got better things to do?
    Roy
Yes! I'm going to get serious now.
    Irv
Oh, no!
    Roy
It's called *Trapped Feelings*.

Trapped Feelings

Loneliness! I feel lonely. I've been writing, if I should be so bold, poetry. It may not be good poetry, but it's different than prose. Prose is written in long lines across the paper, sometimes in volumes and volumes. Poetry is written in short lines, one after the other with spaces between. But that's neither here nor there, so let's move on.

Good poetry expresses feeling! If I'm talking about how I'm feeling, it's because a large part of aging is how the aged are feeling. My conscious mind is working overtime trying to explain how I'm feeling. Does anybody ever get that? Does anybody ever understand how the aged are feeling? When I'm feeling what I'm feeling, for me the feelings are sometimes impossible to put into words. If I express a bad feeling, the only answer I can expect is, *"I'm sorry about that!"* The fact that feelings are difficult to explain is because *"Everyone is different."* Everyone is different because everyone's feelings are different. If we can't get our feelings across, how are others to know? Feelings are sometimes better able to be explained by poetry, but poetry is not always available to the aged, and sometimes the aged discover they have no other way to express themselves and are forced to *"suck it up."*

Let's say at certain times, I feel trapped. When I'm in that state, there's a life and death urgency to stop that feeling. I do not want to have that trapped feeling. I didn't ask for that feeling. I don't know where that feeling comes from. I'm searching for where it came from to see if I can get another perspective on it, or change my actions to reduce it, or work to achieve a more satisfied attitude to make me more comfortable than I am today to *"change that trapped feeling."* Of course this feeling, I suppose, is what all or most aged people go through. If I knew this for sure, would that ease the strain? To know I'm not alone? Would I accept the adamant rule, that all aged people feel trapped and helpless before coming to the end of life and have difficulty as I do as to what to do?

I'm reminded of my mother who was in a senior living facility confined to a small room with another person only partially aware. My fully intelligent mother must have felt trapped, and hoped moment-by-moment she'd die immediately. I feel I know how she felt and feel badly about her situation that's fast becoming mine. I also know, having lived through my mother's experience, that my offspring are heavily into their own lives and can't help their only existing father, just as I couldn't help my only existing mother. What am I supposed to do, then, buy the *"suck-it-up"* plan? Not knowing how to lose *"trapped feelings,"* I'm forced to *"go with the flow."* That means putting up with the pain while struggling to find a solution, to try to understand the problem and affect a cure, change my attitude, or do something, but I don't know what to do to escape that trapped feeling. That's why for now, *"Suck it up"* and *"Go with the flow"* apparently are as beneficial as it gets.

Irv
Can't you write about something more pleasant? Who wants to hear your troubles?
Roy
I am the aged. At least you know that's what I have to say!
Irv
Can't you tell us something more agreeable?
Roy
I could tell you about pleasant experiences in the past, but I've already written 30 books on that subject. To

really know who I am, you have to look at both the good and the bad. In fact, everything in our life has its opposites. Good as related to bad, up to down, in to out, over to under, close to far, high to low. Without the opposites, good, up, in, over, high and close could never be understood.

Irv

Hey! Here comes something good. High Nancy, Eloise and Koo Koo Kakootchna! Hi, girls, howz it goin' wit da' carryin' ons?

Nancy

We're back from just having competed in the Norwegian-American-Lithuania balance beam champ-ionships. Me and Eloise for the United States, and Koo Koo Kakootchna for Lithuania and a few little nobodies from ours and two other countries.

Eloise

Norway tried to keep Lithuania out of the competition, but Lithuania found an almost obscure section of the gymnastic rules allowing Lithuania to compete. Nancy and I didn't care one way or the other.

Roy

No shit! Well who won?

Nancy

Well, of course, I did, but I can't help that!

Eloise

Nancy finished her final balance beam leap with her spectacular balance beam gymnastic trick called the *front running back-1½ ending with a double twist* while flashing a bright smile and scoring the perfect total of 300.00 points. I got second, because when finishing the same twisting trick, I was looking straight ahead, expressionless, with an almost perfect score of 299.00 points, and Koo Koo finished the same twist, coming in third while looking the tiniest bit cross eyed – not her fault of course – with a score of 298.00 points.

Roy
That sounds like everyone did very well, and you all had just the very best little-old time money can buy. You each must feel positively delighted, smiling, hair combed and pokey-dimpled with yourselves.
Nancy
I am, of course, and I suppose Eloise and Koo Koo are not going to shoot themselves between the eyes as a reaction to Koo Koo's lesser final outcome score. Or the fact that they probably feel the tiniest disappointed not being perfect like me in the inner and most fundamental part of their being. *(Nancy, Eloise and Koo Koo. Speaking in union.)* Ta-ta! See you when the tundra thaws, releasing more methane and carbon dioxide into the air, thereby increasing fires and global warming.
Roy
Ta! Ta!
Irv
Ta-ta! Well, Roy, had any dreams lately?
Roy
Right you are if your think you are! Get ready for *Nighttime - Dream #5.*

Nighttime – Dream #5

At four in the morning, my bedroom window with the view looking down over my sloping grass yard with mature sycamores and oaks aligning a narrow creek, I was blaringly jolted awake by the sound of a loudly ringing telephone blasting off in my ear. When it didn't ring a second time, it came to me I had dreamed only one loud telephone ring and began wondering why I dreamed only one and what was that all about?

What instantly flooded my mind was a surprise telephone call I'd received the former day from Lili. Lili is my 60-year old middle daughter living with her husband, Ernie, a hundred or so miles north of San Francisco. That was the end of the short dream. A single ring of the telephone and deep silence.

Irv
What I know about dreams is da da! (Nothing)
Roy
I've always known most dreams spring from recent happenings in the dreamer's life, which the one dreaming has not yet processed. Earlier that day, my talk with Lili took me by surprise. What transpired were serious conversations, but some about reminiscences augmented with humor.
Irv
You're not done, are you?
Roy
No! Dreams seem to inhabit an unfamiliar world, because what happens or doesn't happen in the dream world seems to have nothing to do with real life – unless you are intuitive and make wide comparisons and trust those as true. The telephone ring was all that my inner person

needed to bring up our conversation and give me the time my bottom-line organism needed for closure.
Irv
No shit! I can't wait to hear what you'll scramble my mind with next!
Roy
How about an essay-poem about why these days I find myself swearing?
Irv
I can't think of a worse topic!
Roy
OK! Then, here it is!

To Whom Am I Swearing?

Little is known,
except, I have the
tendency to swear.

> I ask myself
> to whom am I swearing?
> Who is the target?

Swearing is deeply ingrained
in my personality. I can't live
without swearing as illustrated next:

> God Damn it!
> Asshole!
> Shit-faced son-of-a-bitch!
> Stupid motherfucker!
> Get the fuck out of here!

I'm sure I'm my own target
and ask myself!
Why? Why? Why?

> It sounds like I'm unsettled or
> disillusioned with myself.
> What I thought was right in life
> was wrong and appears unresolved.

I ask myself, *"Is disillusionment so bad?"*
I answer,*"No!"* Then,*"Yes!"*

> *What's the disillusion?*

What I expected to be in my life wasn't.

What did you expect?

I never had the chance to find out.

Why?

Because at an early age
I couldn't unhook my
self from my *Mother.*
I was never sure who I was.

> *At an early age, nobody does.*
> *You're not supposed to know*
> *who you are or what you*
> *want out of life.*

So?

> *You didn't know what you*
> *wanted and you did the next*
> *step; followed other people's*
> *advice and now you're angry,*
> *because it may not have turned*
> *out the way you wanted, but you*
> *never knew what you wanted*
> *in the first place, so why swear?*

Were it not for my mother-son-
connection, I'm assuming, or I think,
or I didn't have the freedom and
opportunity to plan my own life.

> *But, who knows, without the*
> *mother-son connection, if you*
> *would have made the right*
> *decisions for a good life?*

I'm angry because I never found out.
With this *after it was too late* insight,
at this stage, I'll never know – then die.

> *And that's what makes you swear?*

It's the only idea that makes sense.

> *Then you know why.*

Yes, but I'm still disturbed by it.
> At this age, I'll not get another try
> and that's why I swear.

I swear because in my lifetime
I wasn't able to choose for myself
how my less-disturbed life might
have been lived.

> I'll never know the joys or disasters
> that might have taken place without
> a mother-bound restricted life.

Is that so bad, considering the life you've had?

> Yes and no! How can I answer that?
> My anger is that at 94 years of age,
> good or bad, my life is over and
> I've missed the single opportunity
> to live as I would have chosen.

I'm stuck with myself and can't get off!

Irv
For gods sake, this book won't end here!
Roy
It's a pretty depressing subject isn't it?
Irv
I'd be happier with something a little brighter.
Roy
I'm not going to end the book there. How about
I Am a Leaf?
Irv
We'll try it out. If it doesn't work I'll leave you to the wolves.
Roy
Nicely put!

I Am a Leaf

At the proper time, that is to say
when nature says the stage is right,
and winter is long gone from fall,
with leaves yellow and bright,
and spring with rain, lightning
and thunder have reached their noisy
ends, my little branch from larger
branches sprung, turns a smidgen
red.

    Then with an inner urgency
    grows a little fatter and with
    some compelling resolution, transports
    a growing bud into a glistening
    sprout that develops without asking
    into an ever-larger shape.

There is, of course,
an adolescent size that speaks
of wonders yet to come and
anticipates a future, the likes of which
can hardly be imagined.

Irv

I think that's better. It is like the tree is telling a story, a bizarre idea in itself, with winter over and spring on its way: about a little branch springing from larger branches that grows by turning a little red, an expression of unstoppable energy, that quickly develops into a larger size, the first indication of the miracle of growth about to occur.

Roy
Wow! You just wacked me over the head with a shovel! I had no idea you could sensitively understand heartfelt poems and explain them with such brilliance and accuracy. Are you somebody else? Are you on drugs?
Irv
I don't believe it myself. Did I say that? I didn't know I was smart.
Roy
Well, I wouldn't go that far. You hit a home run on the only poem I can remember after a bunch of strikeouts!
Irv
Thanks a lot, Roy. Sorry I told you to go dink yourself in the butt a few pages back.
Roy
That's OK, Irv. All's forgotten. Are you ready to get serious?
Irv
Whadaya mean am I ready to get serious?
Roy
I've got something deeper in my mind to consider rather than the more oblivious stuff above.
Irv
I already know I don't like it.
Roy
Well, it's going through my head and hard to keep out.
Irv
You're the writer!
Roy
What about *How to Understand the Universe?*
Irv
My mind is too small.

How to Understand the Universe

Understanding the Universe involves at least four fundamentals, the unchangeable parameters or permanent mileposts of *yes* and *no*, the between *yes and no* percentage of likeliness or unlikeliness and the *other*, acknowledging existence by being present, but no indication of how or why. These four elements could be visualized as four bins, *yes, no, between* and *other*. The other is the last bin into which can be placed almost every item in the universe.

For example, the Universe and everything in it, sky, clouds, mountains, oceans, atmosphere, living things, etc., sits in the *other* bin, because, though we all know everything is here because we are part of it and our senses verify it and we have an awareness of it, yet there is a mystery of how or why it got here. Does the whole Universe have consciousness? I have a close friend who thinks it does. Human consciousness also sits in the *other* bin, a notch down or so, though noticing it's in our selves, plants, birds, fish and animals, we still don't know how or why we have consciousness and limited knowledge of when in the living it appeared.

Maddeningly, the *other* is a marriage of *yes* and *no* and *between* because though we, see, hear, taste, touch, feel and cogitate on it, we are in the dark about how or why it all came about. Perhaps there isn't any *"how or why"* and the birth of the universe will forever remain a big accident or strange mystery and all we can do is *"suck it up."* The final diagnosis might be, *"we are part of all that is"*, and at this point we may never find out how we got here or why we're here. If we don't find out, it's probable the rest of all living things don't, either. Another unchangeable fact is that, though I'm aware that many things exist, I may not know about *all* that exists, including how or why.

What I don't know is invisible to me, as it is to others who also don't know. Even though I have even the smallest conviction that what I don't know may exist, I can speculate, or make up stories 'til the cows come home, and must admit to myself, what I don't know is absent from my mind, and it's impossible for me think of anything meaningful to believe out of my own preferences, worries or fantasies.

For me, what I don't know does not exist, and reason tells me what others don't know does not exist for them either. Anything suggested to exist without proof is speculation and must be put into a place of percentages, the *between* bin, either likely or unlikely *(1% to 99%,)* worth thinking out, or not worth thinking out; that is, worth using our limited time, or not worth using our limited time, a good idea to pursue or a bad idea to pursue.

Is it worth studying for a lifetime whether there is another living awareness in the Universe equal or better than our own? Yes, because our own species might be proof of natures past performance, a fact that suggests a greater probability we'd be successful in finding another being with awareness.

Consider a bee flying at a considerable speed, smashing into a wooden telephone pole, and while expiring, going through metamorphosis changing from a bee into a streetcar carrying 47 passengers to a Dodger playoff game on Vin Scully Avenue in Los Angeles. Would that be worth spending your lifetime to prove? There's a difference between intelligent speculation and wishful thinking.

Irv
You've got to be kidding?

Roy
I suspected the sudden switch from thinking about unexciting subjects such as *I am a Leaf* to those like *How to Understand the Universe* might blow your mind.
Irv
Hey! Here comes Nancy and Eloise! Hi, Nancy! Hi, Eloise!
Roy
Hi, Nancy and Eloise! Nancy, some evening I'd like to take you to dinner.
Nancy
Sure! I thought you'd never ask! However, I do have a tale to tell you.
Roy
Hit me with it!
Nancy
Walking past this very spot last week with Eloise, I stopped at the top of this 40-foot bank to tie my shoe when a sudden gust of wind struck me from behind, and I fell down, rolled over and over, side over side, hair in a tangle, in stockings and dress to the bottom of the 40-foot bank.
Roy
That must have been thrilling!
Nancy
When I got up at the bottom, I'd lost a shoe, my stockings were torn and my legs had a few scratches. Other than my clothes being twisted, lipstick and mascara smudged, and a twig with one dry leaf poking out of my hair, I was OK!
Roy
What did Eloise do?
Nancy
She tried to help by following me down, but slipped at the top and did somersaults all the way to the bottom, and looked the same as me when she got up.

Roy
You should write this up for National Geographic!
I'll pick you up at 8:00 PM this Friday evening for dinner.
May I have your phone number?
Nancy
Here it is, typewritten on this ready-to deliver card. Paste that on your forehead, then before our date, look in the mirror. See you then.
Irv
Nancy and Eloise had quite an adventure!
Roy
Wasn't it, though? I do have next the beginning of a little story called *Beginning of an Aside*.
Irv
Do I have to listen to it?
Roy
I'm sure you don't have anything better to do.

Beginning of Aside

There is a singular question that sounds stupid to me. *If nothing is there can that nothing give and receive information?* If it can't, then for it, whatever might exist doesn't exist. Some would say, No! Things can exist even when nothing is known to exist. But if nothing is there, no one can question, *"What?"* That means only living things, like people who have the most awareness, may know that something else exists, but thinking that something exists without knowing it exists is called speculation and not a fact and therefore, not yet either true nor untrue.

People have a brain and inherent methods in their lives for interpretation, and are most aware to give and receive information. A living entity must first *have the information* for there to be any possibility of *giving the information.* Yet, for the nothing that doesn't exist, this is not true, because there is nothing to receive that informative in the first place and no method of telling it.

Question: How much exists of which we have no knowledge? There can only be *hope* for future awareness of something we don't know exists. *(An example of hope for a reasonable answer to the expanding Universe and the mutual attraction of stars in galaxies is the recent discovery of dark matter and dark energy.)* The mathematics of universal expansion brought us that knowledge. Doesn't that twist your pinkie-pie?

Irv
Is your aside finally over?
Roy
Yep! Now, family issues! It is important to universal knowledge and a very old memory from my childhood

that I include the why and wherefore of the danger of an exit from early age from a locked closet.
Irv
Oh, no! Not that!

Family Issue

In 1934, our tiny Illinois house was in the town of Lombard, 30 miles west of Chicago. It was surrounded by five or six undeveloped acres of waist-high weeds. A rarely used, but paved, Fairfield Avenue ran through the forgotten prairie and past our little house, with another across the street. Mother had taken baby David and driven our ancient Chevy to her sister's for a Sunday visit. Dad and I were alone in the house, and I was six years old, playing at Dad's feet in our young child's bedroom while he had the doorknob off, fixing the entrance to a three-foot-square closet door.

While we were both inside the closet, I bumped the door, and it closed quietly with an ominous click. Inadvertently, I had accidentally locked us in a dark closet with a removed knob and no way to get out. Dad was a mature young father and said not a word, but saw the danger of our predicament and immediately put his mind to the task of getting us out. Curiously, the door had been built opening in, so the hinges were inside the closet and Dad, hard-working responsible man that he was, did whatever it took to take three hinges off the door in the dark with his bare fingers. Within a frustrating half-hour inside the darkened closet, and with me stumbling about father's knees, the door finally swung open and we were out.

Dad reasoned his way out of the closet. As luck would have it, hinges were on the inside. Logic determined they should be on the outside so the door would open out, but luckily, such was not the case. Dad saw this unusual opportunity and used his reasoning brain to get us out.

Where does reason come from? I look to science. New discoveries by science are built on reason, and science continues to grow. If I ask myself why, I'd have to say reason progresses only because the cosmic effects of the Universe provide physical facts that never change. Useful inventions are enabled by unchanging conditions inherent in the cosmos. New inventions can only work in dependable conditions, not arbitrary conditions. Reason dictates up is defined only in relationship to down.

There's no way objects would move away or toward gravity, only away or towards the center of the mass of a close object. If a fork falls off the table, it's tiny mass exerts a proportionate pull on the Earth, totally unnoticed by the Earth since it is so much larger. It's easy to predict it will fall toward the center of the earth and not up in the room. It will not fly around and hit you in the eye. With gravity, I can depend on the fork falling toward the center of the earth - the center of the mass. That knowledge is dependable, predictable, trustworthy, faithful, steady and responsible as any other word I can think of to describe the immovable character, so solid, permanent and reliable as *Yes or No.*

Irv
I'm getting sleepy! What did I learn from that ragged little story?
Roy
Of a miniature episode in the life of one extraneous little four-year-old and his father, eking out an existence in the vast plains of Middle America that no one would ever have heard of if it were not for the minor industriousness of an adult infected with writing on such unimportant things.

Irv
Shall I count myself lucky or unlucky?
Roy
Lucky! Of course! Perhaps the next episode will awaken you. The important information necessary to take out of the following list is that the Cosmos, that is the entire Universe, is filled with dependable facts that allow all modern inventions developed by humans to properly operate. They embody reliable conditions that allow ships to sail, planes to fly, trains to run, cars to drive, and submarines to cruise. Without dependable conditions, science and our modern conveniences would be in chaos.
Let's think about the number of
Reliable Cosmic Conditions.

Reliable Cosmic Conditions

Yes – No	Up - Down
In – Out	Gravity
Weight	Leverage
Levers	Electricity
Radiation	Speed of light
Speed of sound	Planetary rotation
Magnetism	Evaporation
Condensation	Speeds
Quantum physics	Atoms
Protons	Quarks
Bosons	Neutrons
Neutrinos	Sun
Moon	Planets
Stars	Space
Atmosphere	Chemicals
Water	Mountains
Ice	Oxygen
Inertia	Wind resistance
other resistances	Water
Exact passage of time	Zero atmosphere

The myriad meaning the rest that's not on this list.

Roy
Irv, wake up! Wake up! Try this one on for size.
Irv
Huh?
Roy
I want you to be knowledgeable about cosmic and human truths that are sometimes at odds with each other. So please read *Cosmic and Human Truth at Odds*.

Cosmic and Human Truth at Odds

(In the middle of the universe there is no up and down. Up as the opposite of down is true only near two or more bodies of matter affecting each other gravitationally. For this essay, up and down are moving away or toward a closer larger mass.)

Other than the explanation above, opposites and comparisons are unwavering: yes as compared to no, as compared to out, off as compared to on, up as compared to down, wet as compared to dry, life as compared to death, and so on and so on. Another name for this condition is called interdependency. Up must be compared to down or it has no meaning. The concept up or down, in or out, fast or slow, is a portion of life's bible.

Except Humans!

Humans are *undependable* regarding many opposites. Most people lack undeniable characteristics. On the planet Earth, up is contrary to down. Some humans don't believe it and accept up with nothing with which to compare it.

Though people are subservient to cosmic rules thought reasonable by many living human beings, they lack beliefs in many of those same, adamant rules. Light and dark, wet or dry, in or out, back or forth, and sometimes similar agreements on ideas like happy or sad, generous or stingy, gentle or rough, cannot be depended upon, because people, being human, have differences in feelings and thoughts about what they mean.

Humans are not dependable, predictable, or reliable in an adamant, irrefutable, irreconcilable, unchangeable way like they are in Cosmos terms. The most important interdependency many do not believe is that life is the opposite of death. I believe being born in clarification terms can be termed as equivalent to yes, and death equivalent to no. For many humans, heaven is equivalent to yes and so with birth we have yes and when we die, some think we have another yes. *(Life after death)*. As I understand it, this belief does not agree with the rules of the Cosmos except perhaps in a much broader sense such as the decaying remains of death provide the necessary components for other types of life.

Therefore, I see the undependable concept of life as the direct opposite of death to be inconsistent with the concept of Cosmic rules of interdependency that in every case, works. Think of all machinery, the structural engineering of all bridges, all wind resistance beneath the wings of birds or airplanes, water beneath cruise ships, earth and rails beneath railroad trains, etc.,

People, being human and undependable, are unable to have the convenience of agreeing with something as clear as yes or no, or up or down, or wet or dry. To humans, many decisions are based on preference, lack of knowledge, fantasy, or what they want to believe true, whatever that may be. Of course most scientists, chemists, inventors and engineers *do* come to agreement in the truths of the cosmos. They have to, or their inventions wouldn't work. The reliability of yes and no are smack in the face examples of all mechanical inventions, ships, trains, planes and cars, blatantly and timelessly used.

I can depend on humans *not* to be dependable. I can depend on people *not* having the same view. I can depend on them disagreeing with anything and everything I hold dear, because they just don't see it that way. I cannot build a science out of different opinions, beliefs and preferences, because not all people believe in the unchangeable concept of yes or no, or up and down, or in or out. In philosophy, most people are not reliable, predictable, trustworthy, steady, faithful or dependable *(except to themselves)*, and many of those people are impossible to agree with. If what I have shown is the case it's because I know what I know. It's obvious, I'm stuck with myself and can't get off? Then I must suck it up and be thankful and realize I'm personally surviving while others are doing the same, and we all may or may not believe we are quietly and calmly disappearing into oblivion.

Roy
Come on, Irv! Get up! You've been asleep since noon!
Have you got narcolepsy?
Irv
What's nark-o-lep-sea?
Roy
Nark means numbness or stupor. Lepsis means attack or seizure. In other words, are you in a numb attack of sleeping or seizure?
Irv
I still don't get it.
Roy
I knew you wouldn't. Narcolepsy is a condition characterized by brief attacks of deep sleep often occurring with cataplexy and hypnogogic hallucinations. At least that's what the Wik says.
Irv
ZZZZZ!
Roy
Moving on: Now, about *Another Single Theory*.
Irv
Blah! Blah! Blah!

Roy
Thank you Irv! It's good to hear what's on your mind. Anyway, since my friend *(not Irv)* says life after death – Heaven – is related to strange occurrences that affect living beings on earth even though no images project themselves, what are we to think? The greatest idea for me is what follows:
Irv
Oh! You have a theory?
Roy
Hold on to your skivvy-shorts! I have another single theory.

Another Single Theory

Anita Moorjani, in her book *Dying to Be Me* states on the cover, *"Heaven is not a place it's a state.* I presume she means state of mind, not state of madness, or state of ignorance, or state of Illinois, or state of dementia. I am intrigued, since she does not make the usual jump, *into heaven,* and that leaves a strong room for the *state of reason.* Heaven is not a place, but a state. Dying without going to heaven is more reasonable. Heaven is a state of preference, optimism and hopeless desire!

In her new book she informs her readers that while participating in a serious operation, Anita Moorjani was unconscious and in a coma near death. The most unsettling question I have is that how extremely conscious she was of how she knew of the most intimate operating room happenings, and at the same time, how strongly she felt connected to the universe. She seems to have lived in whatever the ultimate meaning of life is while fighting unconsciously for life. After she recovered her fears of dying stopped and she was left emotionally content. *(She did not say she was being ushered into a place with that feeling called Heaven.)* Instead of just a state of the mood she was in, it would be good if she volunteered what state she meant. *The state of what?*

Besides being given the miracle of remembering the past and planning the future, humans have also been given the miracle of speech, opposing thumbs, words, writing books and music, as well as the miracle of ingenuity and figuring things out for themselves. Another miracle might be when the time is right, life is over and it's the proper time to go, 80% of us would more willingly slip into death rather than continue with life and its consequences and sleep peacefully in the place where we were born – the Cosmos - our familiar home of eternity. Moorjani's feeling of being connected to the universe is more reasonable since it gives humans an incentive to die and stay dead. At least humans would be without the burden and questions of an impossible to imagine afterlife.

This understanding is demonstrated by the innumerable deaths in our past, rather than to live some unable-to-be imagined existence forever in an unknown place thought of as heaven, however long that should be. This is not provable, but seems more reasonable than living forever in an unthinkable mind-altering way.

Another theory: One future humongous all-encompassing black hole evaporates into a nothing so big and powerful, it's beyond our imagination to conceive. It then explodes into a wonderful Cosmos the size of our own, and only after countless billions of years returns to another impossibly big black hole, which again evaporates into nothing, at which time it explodes into another Cosmos similar to our own and keeps doing that over and over creating an endless number of Cosmos' forever and ever throughout eternity. All theories work for me!

Roy
Well, Irv, we've reached the point where you're unlucky enough that I'm about to read my next essay.
Irv
Oh no! You mean I may not want to hear it?
Roy
I won't blame you. It's about my aging and a bunch of *"Old"* stuff.
Irv
You mean I might as well just walk out and slam the door.
Roy
It's OK if you do that. We'll still be friends.
Irv
Speaking of walking out and slamming the door, did you ever take Nancy out to dinner?
Roy
Why, yes, we went out last weekend to *Din-Din-dinamonda Creek,* we had two dinners on the deck of a boat sailing into a river. On our first dinner, we were motoring up and down the river at night watching the shore lights and passing motorists and having wine and fish with buttered mashed potatoes and getting inebriated.

You may not want to hear about my baby near-death experience, but with many books on the subject, discovering it is a forgone conclusion.
Irv
Perhaps I'll go out for coffee!

Baby Doug's Near-Death Experience

As a baby of 18 months for the last several days I'd been sleeping soundly for two or three hours, then awakening for two or more. In those days, sometimes there was nothing for me to do but lie awake in bed. Not sleeping is boring, but when I can't sleep it's unbearable. During the day at my present age of 94 years, my body doesn't operate like it used to. Despite whatever motivation I might have, my energy is rarely up to its task. My legs no longer stride forth with strength and youthful vigor, but feel undependable and painful. I can no longer climb up a ladder to the roof, or clean up the shed, or feel like raking the decomposed granite, *"my substitute lawn!"* My energy is no longer primed for it and so on and so on.

As an adult during a sleepless nighttime, I couldn't help mulling thoughts that led me to discover the possible reason for my mental unrest. Could it have been a near-death experience when I was eighteen months old? When I was ten or twelve years old, my Mother told me when I was very nearly two, I almost died of pneumonia. She said for seven days and seven nights, she held her firstborn son to her breast and prayed with God *(or without God, for she was an atheist)* for his life. Pneumonia was a severe disease in the world at a time with no penicillin or drugs to fight it as we do today.

I've since read that severe traumas occurring before a growing baby's first memory can cause severe emotional complications in later life. I can imagine myself at eighteen months old: how I would I have felt at that stage of my life? I'd probably have thought the following. *1 – I'd have felt a high bodily temperature and been tearful and uncomfortably subdued. 2 – I may have had a sore throat, headache or sick stomach. 3 – I'd been off my feeding cycle and probably lost my appetite. 4 – I'd have been unconsciously aware something was vitally wrong. 5 – By closeness to my mother's body, I'd have felt her anxiousness about the possible loss of her only son.*

It might be a truism to say since the brain is divided into two sections, practical and feeling, and a baby with a still undeveloped practical side facing a traumatic event *(almost dying)* could experience problems in later life. Since no memory occurred, it would be impossible for therapists to help an individual so afflicted.

But, I might ask if the feeling side of the brain might also have been sufficiently undeveloped to provide a source for future help from the feeling side of the brain. If the answer is yes, I might have to *"suck it up"* and steel myself for the inevitable. If the answer is no, I might relieve myself of this burden.

This feels right to me and if it is, the next question is what can I do about it? I quit for the night and early the next morning it came to me – the above analysis was *wrong!*

At 94 years old, when the specific time of my future death is still unknown, reason tells me death will be relatively soon. Any increase in strength from my near-death anxiety might have had a profound effect on the way I conducted my entire life. Perhaps early-undeveloped *near-death feelings* rather than *near-death memory* was the probable source of my mental unrest.

Today I was asking what was bothering me in life that I didn't know. Yesterday, upon awakening, I thought I had come to terms with my answer, having dealt with only the left side of my brain *(memory)* and not the right side *(feelings)*.

In life and in general, I had determined the overwhelming and philosophical relationship between opposites or some of the truths about the cosmos: the size of atoms as opposed to the size of the universe, the size of a grain of sand as opposed to the largest size of universal matter, the striking of a match as opposed to the burning of all the stars, the fact that moving *away* from matter is always determined by it's opposite, getting *closer* to matter. Hot is known by cold, in is known by out and life is known by death. All opposites are consistent. If there is a left hand without a right hand, there is no understanding. Left hand cannot be understood by comparing it to another left hand.

In checking life and death, Life is understood by death and death is understood by life. Where there is no death, there is life. Where there is no life there is death. Where awareness is gone, there is death. Where awareness is present, there is life.

What I have described is both the intellectual and practical side of life as against the feeling side of life.

Feelings are also subject to opposites. There are many kinds of feelings, such as I'm feeling exhausted. I'm feeling refreshed. I feel satisfied. I feel unsatisfied. I feel in love. I feel hate. I feel disgusted. I feel satisfied. I feel calm. I feel agitated!

To clarify, where there is life, there are feelings. Where there is death, there are no feelings. Where there is life, there is awareness. Where there is death, there is no awareness. Considering the entire Universe, since there exists infinitely more non-awareness than awareness, and infinitely fewer feelings than the absence of them, we have an entire world made up of infinitely more death and unawareness than life and awareness. Where there is memory, there is life. Where there is no memory, there is death.

And yet despite the great quantity of death and therefore non-awareness and lack of intelligence, the Universe retains a strong sense of organization such as universal expansion, consistency of the rotation of planets and the sun and their orbits being pulled this way and that by planets and other debris traveling unimpeded through space, having been struck by heavier matter and moving by inertia. Could that be the result of an accident and is just what normally happens when a tiny spec of nothing, such as our baby cosmos, blows up into what we understand as our expanding Universe, or do our imaginations allow us to create a living brilliance that could organize all the components of the Universe including atoms, elements, fire, empty space and matter to create that of which we are aware? I guess I'll have to throw that in the *"I don't know!"* bin.

Irv
Well that was hard to hear!
Roy
It's the only thing on my mind these days.
Irv
I'm glad I'm somebody else.
Roy
I'm glad you are too.
Irv
Irv! Here's Nancy! Hi, Nancy!
Nancy
Hi, Irv! How's the old carryin-' nons?
Irv
Followin' my nose! Where's Eloise?

Nancy
Over there! Standin' pigeon-toed with her dress blowin' ever which-a-ways, shy and wanton!
Irv
Hi, Eloise! Why are you pigeon-toed and shy?
Eloise
I guess from all the photographs!
Roy
For fun today, Nancy and Eloise just parachuted off the New York World Trade Center, the tallest building in America.
Irv
Wow! How high is it?
Nancy
It's 1,776 feet high! Our sponsor suggested we think before we jump!
Eloise
For instance, he insisted we put on our parachutes before we jumped!
Roy
That must have been quite a thrill!
Nancy
Yeah! It was! There's a big square pool below, you know!
Irv
There is?
Nancy
Any fool knows that!
Eloise
I knew!
Nancy
No terrible streetcar wires to tangle your parachute lines.
Roy
That must have been gratifying!
Nancy
It was! We've got to get going! We've got to see a banana about appealing.

Roy
Say hello to the banana!
Irv
Roy must have something to do that's better than that quip.
Roy
I think so. Try *Awareness* on for size.

Awareness

What is everything that doesn't care? Answer: anything in the Universe that's not alive! That includes gases, clouds, poisons, rocks, water air, mountains, energy and so on.

Why don't they care? They're missing the parts necessary for bringing caring to life: no feelings of self, no intelligence, no sense of right or wrong, no nervous system, no ability to know, etc.

Does the sun care if your child has a cold? Does the moon care if you had a sleepless night? Does the water care if you had a fender-bender? Do black holes care if you got a D on your math test? Does dark energy and dark matter care if you're hungry? Etcetera.

Living things have the capability of caring.

But things not living are incapable of caring!

Do dead remains of living beings have more capability of caring than a stone? I live – I care! I used to live, but I died. Now I can't care!

If so, how do the dead remains of once living things care?

They don't! Evidently living remains that are now dead have the same lack of caring as anything not alive. For instance, like the same ability to care as a stone.

In the category of once-alive entities, now dead means for them the idea *to care* no longer exists.

Considering the whole Universe, from the standard of

caring, what is the percentage of non-caring dead matter to caring living matter?

If this is too hard to compute, what's the percentage of non-living, dead matter in our solar system *(the sun and eight planets and their moons, comets, asteroids, cosmic dust, etc.)* to the living matter in our solar system of all living things?

My guess would be the percentage is about 99.99% dead matter to 0.01% living matter. *(Or 99.99% unawareness to 0.01% awareness)*

What is the percentage of living matter that can write books, make computers, compose symphonies, invent cars, etc., to living matter that cannot do any of these things?

I'd guess about one species out of 99.99% of the entire range of other living species.

If discovered living species on other planets might have miracles that humans don't have?

Yes! Eagles see more clearly, sharks sense prey at distances under water, whales and dolphins have an understandable language. Duck-billed platypuses have no stomachs, sponges have no brains, mid-ocean volcano explosions *(which can result in tsunamis)* provide life for shrimp, crab and limpets, but credit must be given to humans for the development of nuclear fission, quantum physics, Internet communications, transportation, the Hubble telescope and a trip to Mars.

The Universe, then, including suns, moons, planets, comets, etc., is made exclusively of non-caring matter.

That means matter that is not aware far exceeds matter that is living and aware.

Is awareness a miracle?

Yes!

Are there percentages of awareness?

I'd have to say yes. Certainly there is a huge difference in awareness between the human and an amoeba, a raccoon and a human, or a whale and a human.

But the above analysis only applies to matter, which is a physical part of the Universe.

The above analysis considers the left-brain, but not the right brain, the one devoted to feelings.

In humans, it's been shown time after time, that what a human believes brings about that belief. This includes life after death, heaven, reincarnation, and the belief that crystals have power, as well as astrology, numerous religions and a large amount of what may be pure poppycock. What?

Irv
Well? That's a bit of poppycock!
Roy
A lot you'd know!
Irv
Do you believe that?
Roy
Most of it. But in the following essay, I'll tell you what I do believe, but it's in light of *Earth's Timeline*.

Earth's Timeline

I ran across this piece of interesting information I'd saved on my computer many years ago. I did not record who compiled the information, but surely wish I had. That being the case, it's still my feeling the information is correct and should be part of everyone's education.

The following is based on calculations that one second equals a thousand years.

Earth came into existence	52.5	days ago.
First life forms came into existence	44	days ago.
Life was microscopic until	6.7	days ago.
The Cambrian explosion was	6	days ago.
Amphibians arrived	4.25	days ago.
Dinosaurs arrived	2.3	days ago
Asteroid hits Yucatan Peninsula	18.3	hours ago.
Arrival of Homo sapiens	33	min ago.
Cro-Magnum cave paintings done	32	sec ago.
Mankind traveling in small bands	8.5	sec ago
Jesus Christ was born	2	sec ago.
Present day –	0	sec ago

Roy
Do you believe *Earth's Timeline* is a bit of poppycock?
Irv
I guess not, but it remains surprising that Mankind only arose about a half a minute ago and Jesus was born only a couple of seconds ago.
Roy
Because you bought *Earth's Timeline*, I'm hoping you'll buy *What I Believe*.

What I Believe

1 – The answer to what precipitated the Big Bang at the present moment is unanswerable.

2 – I believe the mainstream of what I read about suns, moons, galaxies, solar systems, and everything I see, hear, feel, know, taste, touch and understand is my reality.

3 – I believe in a regularly expanding Universe. Scientists seem to agree to that, too, and I see no reason to argue with them.

4 – That any surviving living being will not be aware of the end of the Universe because objects like suns, planets and galaxies will be speeding away from each other faster than the speed of light and will be unable to be seen, or the Universe will implode into an immense black hole to eventually evaporate into nothingness. I believe this because I believe a rational scientist whose name I forget who studied the cosmos all his life.

5 – In about 4½ billion years, our dying sun will have expanded and swallowed the earth and other planets and later becoming a dwarf star.

6 – Our massive *Big Bang* explosion either came from an infinite of nothingness, and for me is an unexplainable reason that seems to assume a will or motivation or natural urge. Or it came about as a sensitivity and knowledge that I and all other humans don't have.

7 – I believe reality is what I see, hear, taste, smell, feel and sense or think is real, like mountains, oceans, tsunamis, hurricanes, tornadoes, etc., and all other scientific facts mostly agreed upon by renowned scientists.

8 – I believe it's possible to imagine ideas or scenarios impossible to bring into existence or realize in an actuality that may or may not occur.

9 – I believe nobody can receive or express all information, though some information and distribution is everywhere, like the wind.

10 – I believe humans might imagine ideas or scenarios that do not exist and if that's, possible, though unconfirmed, they may or may not exist.

11 – I believe some persons think they possess inner knowledge, or some kind of consciousness after they have died. A relentless thought. Life is what it is.

12 – Inner knowing is for me as simple as night and day, but provokes questions difficult for me to answer.

13 – I believe whatever doesn't occur to me is totally absent from my being. If I never heard of it, for me it's gone and doesn't exist.

14 – I believe if a human believes something better lies ahead for them, even if they don't know what it is, then that person has positive feelings within his body and derives a benefit from it, even though it may never occur again. For him, the present is good only because of that way of thinking.

15 – I have a personal friend who had a complex type of knowing that within a short period of time was proved to be true. He did not agree that the idea was the result of his own reasonable thinking, but that another type of intelligence *(God or Great Forces of Nature or other indefinable entity)* knew this intimate situation in detail

and to him verified its truth.

16 – I asked who knew the intimate situation as well as he? Only he did. Who could best answer their question? He could. Who knew the least about their intimate situation? His answer was friends, relatives, God and the Great Force of Nature and so on.

17 – Who was the real source of both a difficult and questionable answer? The person who asked the question.

18 – The knowledge of what was projected and what finally happened occurred after both could be shown.

19 – My question: Why leap to the answer of some mysterious foreign entity that proposed it? He may have a mysterious and foreign answer that may be wrong, though now must be considered.

20 – You might answer because the epiphany involved too many unlikely coincidences!

21 – Some answers seem to be related to a preference for coincidences related to *personal trials,* or something I don't know what.

22 - If your questions come from *"personal trials,"* rational thinking is lost and you begin to allow the concept of the philosophy of astrology, birthstones psychics, the paranormal and the non-rational advice given in the olden days in *"The Tibetan Book of the Dead."*

23 – This condition might fall into the category of near-death patients reporting witnessing their own operations out of body from high in the corner of the operating room, or the beginning of the Universe from virtually nothing, or

the mysterious arrival of both life and consciousness, or the miracle of the five senses and feeling; or in near-death experiences the overwhelming ecstasy and willingness to enter death, or the solution of personal problems involving what appears to be unusual coincidences.

24 – I believe it's necessary to give full credit to things I see, feel, think and am motivated about and understand.

25 – Each human knows what his or her own kind of consciousness is and no one else does.

26 – The human kind of consciousness has to do with two sources: Intelligence: the source from five senses, and feelings, the difficult to explain sources from dreams, love, orgasms, hate, including those who've reached a unique understanding from automatic writing, poetry and music.

27 – If there is another kind of consciousness of which we are as yet unaware, and those who've died can't answer if there is another kind of consciousness, there isn't any.

28 – Can humans, once dead, communicate with the living or between themselves? No!

29 – Is consciousness personal for all of the different Tom, Dick and Marys? Yes!

30 – After death I believe the items below are lost forever. There will be no happiness like catching a big wave in the ocean or having a hamburger when hungry? There will be no delight such as making love to a loving mate? There will be no love, or feelings and knowledge as powerful as we have alive on Earth? There will be no ugliness as there is on Earth? Etc., etc., etc.

Irv
Well, that was an eye-opener!
Roy
Didn't you like it, though?
Irv
Except the parts I didn't understand.
Roy
What parts were those?
Irv
Those parts are 1 through 30.
Roy
You mean you didn't get any of it!
Irv
I didn't say that.
Roy
Would you like to know some reliable Cosmic items?
Irv
No! I don't think I would.
Roy
Here they are!

More Reliable Cosmic Conditions

Yes – No
Up - Down
In – Out
Gravity
Weights
Leverage
Levers
Electricity
Electromagnetic speeds
Speed of light
Speed of sound
Planetary rotation.
Magnetics
Evaporation
Condensation
Speeds
Quantum physics
Atoms,
Protons
Bosons,
Neutrons,
Neutrinos
Sun
Moon
Planets
Stars
Space
Atmosphere
Chemicals
Water
Mountains
Ice
Oxygen
Inertia

Wind resistance
Water resistance
Other resistances
Exact passage of time

Irv
What was that all about?
Roy
That was a partial list of all the dependable things the well-organized Universe has to offer us as vital elements our human scientists can use to put workable inventions into constructive *(or destructive)* use.
Irv
Shall I be happy or sad?
Roy
Both, for the truth is in the middle between happy or sad.
Irv
You've got to be kidding.
Roy
Take it or leave it, then try this *Poem* on for size.

Poem

Why are you trapped behind those bars,
my friend?
> *I trapped myself.*

A novel idea, but to what gain?
> *This way I do not have to see the face of God.*

I see. And is that so bad, the face of God?
> *I don't know, I have never seen him.*

Look, then!
> *Are you God?*

No.
> *I don't know where to look.*

Why don't you want to see the face of God?
> *I am afraid He will demand something of me.*

And if he does?
> *I shall not be able to give it to him.*

Why not?
> *He wants my only heart.*

And can you not open it to him?
> *No.*

Why not?
> *I have closed it, forever.*

Why so?
> *If I open it, I shall see the face of Death.*

And is that so bad, the face of Death?
> *Yes.*

Then you are afraid to see the face of God
because he may require you to open your heart.
And if you do, you shall see the face of Death!
> *Yes.*

You stand here, then, afraid of God and Death.
> *Yes.*

You're in a limbo state.

Yes.
You're afraid of God and Death.
Yes.

Irv
That's surely a negative poem.
Roy
I thought you'd like it. It could be your own poem.
Irv
I'm not afraid of God or Death.
Roy
What are you afraid of?
Irv
Missing lunch!
Roy
I have something humorous to tell you.
Irv
I'm glad of that.
Roy
The next essay's a joke!

Laundry and Philosophy

While Marge was taking wet laundry out of the washing machine and putting it into the dryer, I walked in with my book and told her I was reading about *time*. It discussed whether God was making decisions *inside* time like all of us, or *outside* time like from an imaginary place beyond all eternity.

If God were *inside* time, he'd be as surprised as we all are by what the future holds, but *not omnipotent.*

If God were *outside* time, he'd be able to see the past, present, and future of all things and life would be pre-determined and therefore he'd *be omnipotent!*

But, what about free will?

If God is *outside* time and everything is pre-determined, there is no free will and God is *omnipotent.*

If God is *inside* time then God doesn't know everything and therefore, is *not omnipotent.*

At this point Marge put a wet towel over my head.

Irv
That was mildly humorous.
Roy
Did you enjoy the comic break?
Irv
Sort of! Is the next one humorous?
Roy
No! It's about the length of heaven after death.

Irv
How long does the afterlife last?
Roy
I don't know. I've often wondered.

How Long Will the Afterlife Last?

Studies of how long our planet will last amount to a little more than 4½ billion years. But, well before that our dying sun will have expanded large enough swallow up the earth and burn up our entire solar system. If the earth, planets and sun are gone where does heaven go?

Regarding how long the universe will live there are two theories, the first one involves the expanding universe. Stars moving away from us *(wherever the future has us)* will speed away faster than the speed of light and light from future suns traveling at the speed of 186 miles per second, will not be fast enough for us to see them. In other words, stars, if any, will be so far away, light will not travel back fast enough to be seen by other planets, if there are any.

Second theory on the end of the universe: It will implode or collapse into a giant black hole that will last sufficient time in its mysterious swirling heaviness until eventually it evaporates. To where does it evaporate? Will heaven last this long? Where does heaven go when there is nothing? How long is eternity? In opposition to an *existence in Heaven after death*, the incentive to die and knowing the meaning of the universe while slipping into *no life after death* is the answer. Who else has this theory?

Irv
Jesus Maria Sanroma!
Roy
That sounded like swearing!
Irv
It did, didn't it? But it's not. It's the name of a historical pianist.

Roy
I didn't know you were that smart!
Irv
There's a lot you don't know about me. I went to college, you know.
Roy
I did not know that! I would never have expected you retained that amount of schooling. But I do have other information I'd like to get off my chest called *Whole Brain Living.*
Irv
If I have to listen I will.

Whole Brain Living

Encouraging me to believe my thoughts about the absence of heaven after death were two books I recently read called *My Stroke of Insight* and *Whole Brain Living* written by neuro-anatomist Jill Bolte Taylor. At 37 years old, Jill succumbed to a massive stroke that destroyed the entire left side of her brain and she retained only the abilities of the right side. With only the right side of her brain and working with her after her traumatic experience, she found her thoughts were similar to the ecstatic near-death experiences recorded in many former books; a sense of love and connection with the entire universe. This tells me there is a portion in the left side of the brain inhibiting the full expression of the impossible-to-describe feelings of ecstasy, warmth, love and caring produced by a portion of the right side of the brain. Studies show that the human brain can take in only so much of the world. Filters have been miraculously installed to keep information out. Otherwise, the brain would be too saturated to function.

Irv
Well, la de da!
Roy
Weren't you impressed?
Irv
Sort of – if I knew what you were talking about at all.
Roy
Well, how about a story of why you don't know why you're here?
Irv
Can't you think of something easy to think about?
Roy
How about the following:

I'm Stuck With Myself and Can't Get Off

1 – You didn't ask to be born in this world.

2 – You haven't asked to leave this world, but may be compelled to depart with conditions not especially of your own accord.

3 – You also didn't specify the type of world or conditions you'd be entering.

4 – You find when you are here you are in a specialized group with similarities, but unique from every other member.

5 – With human life comes awareness, and if you are aware of the Universe, you can see it exists.

6 – Those without life can't be aware of it because to those not there, the Universe can't exist.

7 – With life, there is awareness and you notice the Universe.

The point is: The Universe without your awareness would not exist. You, being alive and aware is the only reason the Universe exists. It doesn't exist if you are not here to verify that it does. Isn't that sort of curious? The Universe is born on the same day you know it.

Irv
You mean if I'm not here, the Universe doesn't exist?
Roy
Well, it may exist, but if you're not here, you won't know it, so for you, it doesn't.
Irv
I get it. I think.
Roy
The Universe is gone, unless you are around. In a certain way, the Universe doesn't exist unless you are here. If you're not here, it either does exist or doesn't exist. Since

you don't exist, you'll never know and can't care one way or the other.
Irv
You mean the Universe isn't here for me if I'm not here?
Roy
Yes! If you are here, you are responsible to be aware of the Universe! Point anywhere and there it is!
Irv
Well! La de da!
Roy
Take the following dream. You'll love it!
Irv
Oh, no!
Roy
This is dream is about flying over the desert while sleeping. There is meaning somewhere in this wide, wide, world. I've thought about an interpretation, but haven't made much progress.

Dream Flying Over Desert

I find myself sitting several hundred feet in the air on what reminds me of a leather swing seat. I suspect the ropes or cables on either side are connected to an overhead wing that holds me aloft. There is an openly supported metal structure projecting in front of me holding a spinning three-foot diameter, four-bladed propeller that moves me forward. I watch the scenery below, which is unending sand that is billowing somewhere and in others, rolls like a washboard.

I travel like this for many hours observing this interesting, but in the long run a rather boring scene. Then I notice someone far below driving a small, open-topped vehicle that's heading for a large trunked, baobab-like tree that stands alone in the vast, sandy desert. He bumps into it with his vehicle and the tree topples over. The *"someone"* gets out and tries to straighten the tree with its ridiculously wide trunk that towers over him. But it falls the rest of the way over and remains collapsed on the sand.

He goes to the other side and tries to *"right"* the tree, with success, and the trunk plops easily into the watery hole from which it came. The tree is standing upright again, but this time the trunk is more stick-like, even woodier and wider with branches and foliage adjusting accordingly. I fly on. There is more boring desert, but soon I see a green oasis in the distance. It looks like a green island in the wasted sand. And as I approach, I sit in my sling-seat and lower myself to get a closer look.

Presently, I'm flying right next to the dark green foliage and large stone-like wall. Fence-like structures project from the side of the foliage and I fly right next to the greenery and stone-like walls. I'm now closer to the ground and when I awake, I'm precariously close to the stone-like walls. Having looked at the National Geographic recently and seen the multitudinous aerial configurations of sand, perhaps I had not internalized what I was seeing.

Roy
Perhaps the dream helped me fly over this sand to internalize some indefinable experience. What the tree and green *"island"* is, is still a mystery. What do you think this brought to mind, Irv?
Irv
I have an itchy elbow that won't go away.
Roy
Can't you help me with a more serious analysis? Do I have to do all this by myself?
Irv
*No! I think I hear my mother calling me.
Well, to what glorious circumstance do we owe the visit of two of our most respected balance beam champions, Nancy and Eloise?*
Nancy
You are too kind! Hi, Irv! Hi, Roy!
Irv
Nancy, did you and Roy ever go out to dinner?
Roy
I took her to Spruzzo's and we had charbroiled filet mignon served in brandy & peppercorn sauce with a Nicoise salad and a Meyer lemon Margarita.
Irv
Where's Koo Koo Kakootchna, your other Lithuanian balance beam champion?
Eloise
She's in jail for shoplifting and then has to do a month of community service – mopping the floors of K-Mart, I think

Irv
Wow! Is she in jail often?
Eloise
She has a bad habit of stealing unimportant stuff she could really buy. She'll be out of jail next month.
Irv
What month is it now?
Eloise
October.
Irv
That's not too bad, is it?
Nancy
Roy, after you died, would you like to retain your body?
Roy
Let me think about that!

Retaining Myself After Leaving My Body

Do you mean if I had a choice? Judging by history's past experience, I don't believe I'd have a choice. I can witness over and over again that at death, the body, its five senses and brain quickly deteriorate past any self-function whatsoever.

If you're asking if it's important I retain an awareness of my distinct person after I leave my body, I suppose I'd have no choice on whether I did or not. If there was a doubt, I suppose I'd be compelled to go with the flow. I can't imagine retaining awareness, eternal or limited, after death exists, nor if it would be advantageous. After all, one of the definitions of death is loss of awareness. But, if you're questioning whether there is a total loss of awareness, how can anyone predict what's inside a dead human that is similar to an unopened box? But the answer to your original question is no, it's not important I retain a sense of my individual self after I'm dead and leave my body.

Leaving your body after death assumes you have enough awareness after you are dead to leave it or not. Death assumes there is no awareness to leave or not to leave after death. Though, some people claim it with enthusiasm, I must retain a shred, if it's to be that, of doubt. At this point, I do not assume I will have any awareness after I'm death.

If there is no *"self,"* how would we distinguish one of *"the illusions of individuality"* we call ourselves between one another? For after all, each individual is distinctly unique and the definitions of illusions are not going anywhere. You might drop the illusion of individuality, yet the illusion is forever with us. The answer is yes and no. The truth is we could be both an illusion and not an illusion. We are one body of people, but at the same time we are only one critical part of that group called one body. We are part of one body of people but also a specific part of one person in that body. We can or cannot be thought of as a single, permanent illusion. We are always both.

As an example, look inside ourselves. There's water, atoms, protons, neutrons and quarks assembled into a heart, spleen, kidneys, pancreas, liver, stomach, legs, arms, and on and on. Yet we know that each of us in that whole congregation *(the illusion of ourselves)* Doug, or Lili, or Vivi, or Amanda, has a self. Our insides are the *"Oh, so much more!"* than just the name we call ourselves.

Each individual person's sense of oneness was made, like the inside of the body, of parts, or the illusion of individuality or self. The self or the singular name for individuality or illusion is part of what the whole *(or oneness)* of which it is made. It is correct to look upon yourself as both – a reality and illusion.

Roy
I understand death encompasses no awareness. If awareness exists after death, we have no death. If you asked a rock, *"what's the square root of 16?"* and the rock answered, *"four,"* I'd say the rock was smart, alive and aware.
Irv
What if he answered three?
Roy
Then I'd say he was taught wrong.

Irv
What if he was raised in another world where the dead were still alive and he was right and you were wrong?
Roy
Are you trying to confuse me?
Irv
Maybe you're already dead.
Roy
It takes one to know one! Let's go on with *Shadow Life*.

Shadow Life

Shadow life is what you're thinking when not interacting with *Real Life*. *Real Life* is when you're playing your *Real Life* game. For instance: You're in a game of baseball and you're at bat with two balls and two strikes. The umpire just called, *"ball three!"* It's three and two! The next pitch will tell the story. Either you get a hit, or fly out, or you swipe air and strike out. If the game's baseball does that mean, *"game over?"* If it's just a game, probably not; tomorrow's another day. If you've struck out and the game is *health* and life is *terminal,* the game *is* over. If that thought strikes you alone on some sleepless night, you're living in the *shadow* half of the *Shadow Life.*

Since a person has a *Shadow Life,* you may or may not choose to tell anyone about your *"other"* life. To a close friend or colleague, brother, sister, or anyone, you may choose, to say, *"I had a thought the other day,"* and tell them this or that. If you do so, you've told them a piece of your *Shadow Life*. The essence of creativity is contained in your one and only, utterly unique, *Shadow Life*. Dreams are part of the *Shadow Life*. I can never really explain my dreams clearly to another person, or usually to myself. The *Shadow Life* is sometimes difficult to express. Then, of course, there's the *meaning* of the dream, a different chapter, but still involving the *Shadow Life.*

Dividing *Plain Life* into two categories, *Real Life* and *Shadow Life,* allows me to get a more objective look at who I am. When I get up and go to work, I'm in *Real Life*. If I lie in bed sleepily cogitating a dream, I'm in my *Shadow Life*. Some types of cogitating I may call *Introspection*. I guess you might say when I cogitate, I can see myself more clearly and from a different angle. I've learned if I need a solution to something, I think all around it with an open mind, doing the best I can to delineate everything leading to a solution. This will remind me of that, and that will remind me of this. Reminding me and calling attention to what might be contributory to the answer is at least better than not doing so. Such are some of the workings of *Shadow Life*.

(To make a thought clearer, tell someone (even better), write it (even better), draw it (even better), and make a movie (even better).)

The *Shadow Life* is sometimes called *Private Thoughts*. All thoughts, if we choose to look at them are both private and part of the *Shadow Life*. Having a thought is called thinking. We think in the *Shadow Life*. Without thinking, there's a major part missing in human life. Thinking differentiates humans from animals. Thinking is closely related to the concept of I want, which is closely related to doing. Is a man what he thinks or what he does? Or both? Without wanting to fly, there would be no airplanes. Without wanting to travel faster, there would be no cars or roads. Without wanting to cross rivers, bridges would be unnecessary. Without wanting to cure cancer, there would be no attempt for a cure and so on. All these desires come to fruition with a combination of the *Shadow Life* and two simple words - I want. Afterward, there's the doing.

The words, *I Want*, are the source of creative thought that begins in that usually hidden part of all people I call the *Shadow Life*.

Irv
I didn't know that while I was whiling away the time I might have been thinking?

Roy
You might have been, though whiling away time is rarely considered thinking!
Irv
What if you thought you were whiling away the time and you didn't know you were thinking, but you accidently solved a bunch of problems you didn't know you were working on.
Roy
Then you were accidently thinking.
Irv
Wow! How many people can do that?
Roy
You might be the only one. That reminds me of a *Shadow Life* of my episode a year ago.

Shadow Life a Year Later

I was sitting having breakfast at 9:30 AM reading a story about a woman and child caught in the Japanese tsunami. They established a relationship when the woman rescued the child, and soon the child took the place of the woman's own child lost in the flood. After a few years, the child's real mother discovers the child in the mall, but the child decides to acknowledge his rescuing mother as his real mother. The real mother believes her son's story and with great reluctance, wanders away.

At that point, I felt teary-eyed. At first I attributed it to the story, then realized I was crying for myself. What was I crying about? It was about the fact that my own life is over. I'm 94½ years old and have attended the Malibu Senior Citizens luncheon celebration where I realized all these people were at the place similar to where elephants go to die. I wondered why I didn't have real tears and let it all hang out, but I guess that's not my way. Lately, I've been experiencing an existential crisis and it is probable this is part of it. My existential crisis is coming to terms with the fact that my life is essentially over.

I presume, like *The Little Train that Could,* I have to adopt the phrase, *"I think I can. I think I can. I think I can"* until I can't move anymore.

Irv
Well, I think I'm sorry for you!
Roy
Thanks a lot, Irv! I know that while I thought I was whiling away my time, I was really thinking, so I guess sometimes if you feel you are killing time, you can be using time successfully.

Irv
How was that so?
Roy
The existence of the tsunami drifting through my mind, brought tears to my eyes for myself at the age I'd achieved before realizing that old people die like elephants go to die. They die at a senior citizens luncheon with an existential crisis symbolizing their life essentially, is over.
Irv
Let's think about more positive things.
Roy
OK! How about a dream!
Irv
Oh no! Not another one.
Roy
It's called, *Dream with Long Wire*

Dream with Long Wire

I dreamt there was a long, stiff wire tied together every eight to ten feet and hanging from something high, probably a cliff. It was dipping and swooping for a long distance attached to some unknown place far out at sea.

I went hand over hand, like a child swinging on the monkey bars. It seemed easy. My hands didn't hurt. I had strength in my arms. I proceeded, without difficulty.

There was no indication where I was going. I just knew I was going to travel forward, hand over hand, out and down the long, swooping, dipping, tied-together wire.

Presently, due to the dipping wire, the ocean was getting close to my feet and I found the wire and I was going to dip into the water. I was going to get my feet and legs wet. The water had small, choppy waves, indecisive and arbitrary looking, the water unclear, but gray-green with no view into the depths. The day was plain. It had no distinguishing characteristic; a sort of twilight. There were no clouds, but just a plain, dull, uninteresting day, not important to the dream. I don't even remember getting wet.

Eventually, I reached a landing or dock of some kind and discovered a weak spot in the wire that was almost broken and would have plunged me into the water. I tried fixing the wire by tying it together, but wasn't successful.

Irv
We certainly have a good record of your dreams. Thanks for the analysis. I'm sure it did you a lot of good, but what good did it do us readers?

Roy
It's my job to fill the space in a 200-page book. That's the reason why I'm wasting the reader's time. How about a joke? I've got one called, *Another Recent Episode.*
Irv
OK! If I have to read it, I will.

Another Recent Episode

The father organism is on his hands and knees on the floor of the family room and is happily ironing the rug and singing *Whistle While You Work* when his teenage daughter on her way out, hits him on the head with her purse, knocking him ever-so-slowly, knees over t-shirt, into the corner where he eventually comes to rest, hair over his eyes and surprised.

Later - to Marge - the father organism says, *"Now, why'd she do that?"*

Washing dishes, Marge replies, *"You were ironing the family rug with a clothes iron."*

"I know," Father replies, *"but it wasn't plugged in."*
Heavy sigh.

Roy
Did you think that was funny?
Irv
Yeah! That was pretty funny. On a scale of 0 to 100%, I'd give it maybe an 85%.
Roy
Thanks a lot! That's one of the nicest things you've ever said to me. Can we get on to the more important stuff, now? It's called *A Frank Philosophy?*
Irv
I can wait!

A Frank Philosophy

Note: When I was steadily in practice, my houses were the best I could do. I didn't have to establish myself. I was already established. I only took jobs that allowed me to express what I believed, not only about construction, but also about life as a whole. I was in love with my work. I did everything myself: program writing, design, working drawings, specifications, contractor selection and once a week supervision. I make what I think are classic houses and I'm sure you'd enjoy what my clients and I have created.

I don't like the idea that a house has to be ostentatious or eye-catching or have some kind of curb appeal. I don't do that. I try to build a beautiful house fitting sensitively into its site; one the owners are proud to own because it conveniently accommodates their way of life; one they like to come home to because it's beautiful and contains everything they love.

I don't believe people are for houses, but *houses are for people.* If we think that people are for houses, many clients have to adapt themselves to the architect's intricacies. In our house you will not have to do that. Our house is an understated *background* for you, your children, guests, activities, books, music, artwork, furniture and anything else you'd like to bring into it. The new environment will not intrude upon the senses, but is quietly beautiful; an environment where a sudden delight of the senses awakens you to how lucky you are to be in the place you are.

Some houses look as if the architect was forced to establish himself in his own eyes and, therefore, in the eyes of others. They are usually showy and pretentious. *(One example would be a house near the ocean in the shape of a wave, or a house in the mountains looking like a boulder.)* We get it! I'm tired of looking at them. I wish they'd go away. In fantasy, if not in actuality, my houses love secret places; they're lost in the woods and covered with vines; gone from the world, and the owners are snug, secure and in love with the place where they are. This is my idea of what the author's house will do for you.

Irv
Well, whoop de dooooo!
Roy
I've tried to be as modest as required and inconspicuous and less important than I think I am.
Irv
Yes, I think you've done the best you can.
Roy
If I don't think of me having done the right thing who'll have thought so? That reminds me of my next eloquent exposition called *Thinking the Whole*.

Thinking the Whole

I just ran into a quote by Mark Twain & quoted herein:

"It ain't what you don't know that gets you into trouble, it's what you know for sure that just ain't so."

That means whatever *you "know for sure"* should be taken with a grain of salt. Like everybody else, I have thoughts, hopes, desires, intelligence *(or lack thereof)* and motivation. It is better to be aware of the *"whole,"* rather than a part, and applies to life as well.

Sandwiched as I am with my own personal brand of talent, passion and motivation, it's imperative I know as much of the *"whole"* as I'm able. The whole of being an architect involves; A, the client, B, the site, C, the contractor, D, the Building Department, and E, my own desires, enthusiasms, creative ability, knowing the *"whole"* and who I am in the world. It's necessary I don't get into trouble because *"I know something for sure."*

Irv
Can't we get on with something more important? Like an essay with cosmic proportions: one that makes me want to stand up and view life from an entirely different perspective?
Roy
Yes! I think I've got the one essay that will forever change your life. One that will make clear to you all the inclinations of positivity of which you yearn to bring into clear focus; something you've always known but as yet hadn't clarified. It's called *Bigger Than the Bug.*
Irv
Bug? It's about a bug?

Bigger Than the Bug

In all cases, the architect must be bigger than the problem. Something I'd previously written is a story that will better illustrate the point.

I had just gone for a morning jog, and on returning, was doing a few exercises on the patio when I noticed a little black dot moving slowly and quietly across my concrete slab patio. I wondered what kind of creature was way down there while I was way up here swinging my arms. It was just a tiny black dot moving hesitantly but steadily in what seemed a totally arbitrary direction. Wanting a better look, I leaned way down from my great height and put my hands on my knees and nose within a foot of the living thing, and discovered it was a tiny bug wavering slightly as it moved in a timeless way.

As I watched him, I caught a glimpse of eternity. This harmless creature existed right in front of me, not knowing how he got in to this world, yet doing something that nature carefully designed him to do, living and making decisions for reasons completely unknown to me. And here I was, existing as a human and making my way through the world, with reasons just as completely foreign to him; going about my business as nature designed me to do. On our Earth, the beetle and I were the same. It was our job to do the things nature had designed us to do. So I decided to be here and do what I was capable of doing including jog-walking, exercising, laughing, feeling sadness, architecture and catching glimpses of eternity while having all the other human strengths and frailties. Relative to his world, the beetle was doing the same. I love the bug as I love myself.

Talking to the Bug

Like asking patio boulders where they'd prefer to be, I made up a conversation with the bug. *"Where are you going way out here in this concrete desert? It will take you days to reach the edge of the slab, and if you do, what then? Fall three inches to dirt and a jungle of pebbles and stones, tangled weeds and dangerous predators like ants and spiders? You're hopelessly lost in the middle of my twenty-foot-square slab."*

The bug might reply, *"I know nothing of you. I'm alive. I move. I exist. I'm minding my business, doing my thing, calmly walking with passion, fear and curiosity; feeling my way, nosing this way and that, using my twenty-eight legs like oars on a boat and wiggling feelers that tell me of foreign objects, leaves, twigs or the air's motion, its temperature, and hopefully find what I ultimately desire: food, life and my mate's bouquet."*

Though I was doing only one house in a world of billions, it was necessary I be bigger than the bug.

Before We Do Anything We Must Have Integrity.

People like integrity. The bug is a living entity and all living creatures *(except some humans),* have integrity. Creatures can't be changed as to who they are. Permanently enclosed in their body, they can't get off. He can be brutalized by fate or an unthinking ego, but as a human, architect or not, I'm bigger than the bug, and fortunately for the bug, may have something the bug does not have: compassion. As all living creatures with the exception of some humans, the bug breathes integrity.

Inanimate things of the world, like stones, water and sand also have integrity. They are our brothers and sisters and provide the home in which we live. They can be nothing else. They have no ability to change themselves. They don't fool us. They do not bear false witness. In fact, everything in the Universe *(excepting some humans)* has integrity. I think all people like integrity. We can depend upon integrity. Integrity is at the core of trust. A cat is always a cat, an elephant always an elephant, a duck-billed platypus always a duck-billed platypus. Living and non-living things are the ultimate in reality and, irrevocably, are what they are.

To Be an Architect
One lesson of the *"bug"* tale is that if you want to be in control, it's better to be in control with compassion and empathy and to be bigger rather than smaller. As an expert in design and construction, an architect must be bigger than the land, bigger than the client and bigger in understanding of the governing laws, because size, intelligence, talent and compassion are controlling factors.

Out of control is unacceptable. If I'm not bigger than the bug or the problem, I'm not in control of what happens. For the client to accomplish his ultimate goal, the architect must have integrity and be bigger than the problems, or *"bigger than the bug."*

Roy
There were two living beings on my patio, a tiny bug and myself. We have been created by the *Universal Force or God,* have integrity and are both doing what we're designed we do. Who's to be the most commended?
Irv
You are both to be equally commended.
Roy
Thank you, my good and true friend, but do you think humans will agree?

Will Humans Agree?

Where humans are concerned, it is a truism to say there is no agreement that people of the world will totally agree on the meaning of answers like yes and no, do or don't do, will or won't, jump or don't jump, cut or don't cut, etc. *(When I was born, the Earth's population was 2 billion people. Now it is just under eight billion people and increasing in numbers as time goes by.)*

Death for humans is about what lives and what does not. After death, the body decays into standard molecules and chemicals of earth and a tiny portion of the Universal Cosmos. The powerful loss is awareness.

Some say the spirit remains after death with its spirit and soul. I only partially agree.

Webster says, *"Spirit is the inspiring principal of dominant influence, or soul."* All living beings have life, soul and spirit. I give all non-living matter including earth, moon, rocks, mountains, etc. a spirit or soul. The soul is the spiritual part of man, but can also be understood as the spiritual part I give to the soul of matter. If mankind who lives and matter *(without life)* have spirit and soul, they need someone to be aware of it or remember it. If no one is experiencing or remembering it, the spirit and soul can't exist. Someone might say the spirit exists, even though no one knows it exists, but there is no preliminary evidence that its true, promoting the question, does it exist if no one knows it exists? In my opinion, for that unreceptive entity, it doesn't!

When someone says there have been many knowledgeable humans that have arrived and died in the past 80,000 years who recognized one or more spirits, we could throw that into a bin called the collective unconscious. In Jungian psychology, the part of the unconscious mind derived from ancestral memory is common to all humankind and is distinct from the individual's accessible conscious mind. Since all the people in the collective unconscious were dead before present events, they can't experience spirits present of our century.

If you're going to discuss the question, *"is there life after death?"* you have to take into account the most important consequence inferred. If there is life after death, what kind of life is meant, general life, like everything living on the planet, or a continuing of the former individual's life? To approach an answer to that, we apply reason, since reason is another miracle integrated into all human life to a greater degree than all other living entities.

When dead, it's easy to see the human brain is no longer operating, so its ability to reason is impossible to access. No longer operating are the mind, self and five senses.

There are untold billions of formerly alive people, animals and beings of the past who have died and none have come back. This documents an immense list proving the permanence of death.

It must be kept in mind that though we might imagine what the tribulations of life for humans in the far-distant past might have been like, there is little factual knowledge or written history of how that might have been. Especially concerning life after death. We know very little of their 6,000-year-old concerns. According to Carl Jung, we do carry an inner knowing of what he called the *"collective unconsciousness."* It is described as *"a collection of knowledge and imagery every person is born with and shared by human beings due to ancestral experience."*

Common, everyday remembering can sometimes be confused with the remembrance of a person's spirit. Spirit might be confused with the collective unconsciousness, or what we remember might make a difference in our lives, and we might call what we remember of his or her spirit influencing us, but it doesn't affect the question of whether or not there is life after death.

Roy
I'm sorry for going on and on about life after death.
At 94 years old, I have to either get it in my mind that the ultimate answer to life after death is going to happen when I die, or that which is in my mind already – there is no life of the exact same individual after death.
Soon I will be tired of the subject and will automatically shut down on the whole topic.
Do you think that's a good idea?
Irv
I'm sick of the whole subject! Every living thing dies, turns to earth that grows a surplus of living things, but we don't know what!
Roy
I'm sick of it, too!
Irv
I'm not aware of much of anything while I'm filled with life.
Roy
Neither am I! Let's talk about *Easier Things*.

Easier Things

I believe the sun will come up tomorrow because I've lived for over 80 years, and during that time I've been there while it came up day after day.

One time, our Dance Group hiked to the top of Bony Ridge Mountain near Malibu and we sat among the morning grasses and watched the sun silently creep above the horizon. It was magnificent! It has a good track record. It's been doing that for 4½ billion years. I believe the sun will come up in the morning.

The moon, too! All my life I've observed the moon going through its normal phases, zero to crescent to quarter to half to three-quarters and finishing with a glorious full moon, illuminating all the windblown grasses and wheat fields. In the full moon's light, animals roam the darkness to feed. As in a dream, snakes slither purposefully in the night for food, and with yellow eyes, owls give an after-dinner hoot. Mountain lions stalking prey prowl under the rising moon.

I believe in rainstorms, snowstorms, sleet, fog, clouds, wind, etc., because I've either experienced them or seen them on TV.

I believe in TV because I can see the screen, and I believe in computers and transportation systems like cars, because I have driven one to Staples.

I believe in ocean pollution, diminishing shark populations, shellfish, barrier reefs, extinction of human and animal species and what seems an almost human disregard for the world, including population, pollution, global warming plants, animals and minerals.

I have observed the do-good organizations such as the Red Cross, Salvation Army, Goodwill Industries, The Sierra Club, and those individuals who have compassion for the rapidly deteriorating and increasingly pathetic condition of the planet Earth.

The Universal Force

But it's easy to believe in things right in front of your face. But what about the concept of God, the ambivalence toward organized religions, the arguments for and against abortion, the paranormal, natural evolution, politics and life after death?

I believe in a *Universal Force,* which some may call God, that allows all of which we are aware and all of which we are *not* aware to exist.

Though it's against all reason, I imagine the Big Bang; beginning at a point so small scientists call it *"singularity"* and then an apparent explosion so immense it created the whole universe and everything in it, parts of which we know and parts we don't know. All within an immense cold, empty space so large, expanding dimensions are only relative distances between physical bodies that are continually changing.

Now draw an imaginary line around the whole universe, and notice our galaxy is wherever you'd like it to be, and our planet is within that galaxy and also inside that circle. Notice, too, that *we* are on our planet and this forces us to admit we humans are a small extension of the Big Bang. *"Star stuff!"* as Carl Sagan would call it. I am part of the Big Bang whether I choose to be or not! Everything is the result of the Big Bang, including me and all plants, animals and minerals.

Parallel lines, like railroad tracks that never meet. I have to accept that fact.

Fortunately, cutting matter continually in half to find the smallest building block of the universe is no longer necessary. Scientists have now determined virtual particles appearing out of the void are introduced spontaneously without any nucleon or other strongly reacting particle being present.

I can always add one to the largest number I'm capable of imagining.

If a God, great in his purpose, designed the Big Bang, I have to ask who made that God and who made the second God, and third, ad infinitum until what is left is only another question: *"who made that one?"* If that non-answerable question were true, I'd have to accept that fact, too

Parallel lines that eventually meet or discovering the one and only final God is unreasonable. I have to accept that fact.

It is reasonable to believe that some things in my universe have no finite solutions. Some things are insolvable.

What is, is! And whether I think it's a miracle or not, I have to accept that fact, too.

There are questions I have with absolutely no answers from me or any living or un-living creature to be found.

Life After Death
I bought a refrigerator and was told the light goes out when I closed the door. Imagining no other way to test the state

of light, how would I really know the light was out when I closed the door?

I took a chair and put it down in the kitchen and sat down to get a close look at the edge of the refrigerator door. While closing it, I watched it carefully with keen eyesight and was unable to see if the light really went out. I came away with no closure; no assurance I was not wasting electricity or my time. I wasn't sure whether it went out or not and have reached no indication either way; no sign of relief that I know the truth of what's happening. Of course, my trust in the character of the refrigerator remained intact.

If my life were the refrigerator, and closing the door was death, and the man told me the light *(my life)* was supposed to stay on and perhaps be more brilliant than before, how could I be sure?

Those who've had near-death experiences are convinced there is life after death; however, they were still alive when they came to know that truth. They weren't dead like the raccoon I saw lying inert on the highway for a few months, whose body was quickly turning to dust.

When people like my mother and father have passed on to unequivocal death, and let's say after a couple of years, how do I know they are still living the good life in the hereafter? I don't!

What then is this *"through eternity"* everyone talks about? There is no eternity except the large, small or medium changes that a particular person left, minimally or maximally, upon our present-day world. Thank you, Mr. Thomas Edison. Thank you, Mr. Henry Ford. Thank you, Mr. Mark Twain.

The condition is similar to parallel lines that never meet, the division of matter resulting in yet something to divide, and being assured that one Deity is the absolute and final God that made everything, I can never know and I have to accept that fact.

Serious Prayer

Serious praying is profound hope that calls out to all known and unknown sources of aid.

Praying your child recovers from a severe illness or that you don't get killed or injured in the war or your leaking boat stays afloat until you reach shore are worthy of serious prayers.

For all serious problems, I would pray to beneficial forces for my recovery, to doctors, nurses, high-end equipment, family, and others willing to aid while making up a useful portion of the Universal Force.

If I call the Universal Force *"God,"* I would be praying to God.

Prayer is making it known I need help. It's possible I may never know the source of what aids me, but the more signals I send, the more help I pray I might get. More loving brains praying are better than fewer loving brains praying.

This thought is at least a thought it's a pleasure to believe.

As Ted Turner's father told him, *"Early to bed, early to rise, work like Hell and advertise."*

Someone said, *"Pray to God, but keep your powder*

dry. Don't pray to God to keep your powder dry for you."

Unserious Prayer

To win the big game, forces must be in place and team members must be healthy, motivated and well-practiced, then prayer is unnecessary.

There's a difference between reasonable and unreasonable praying.

If team members are unhealthy, unmotivated and unpracticed, reasonable praying degenerates into wishful thinking. Even if it's really hard, wishful thinking rarely helps.

Roy
Say hello to my close friends, Nancy and Eloise, balance beam world champions of the first order!
Irv
Hi Nancy and Eloise, win any world championships in the balance beam lately?
Nancy
Yeah! We won first and second in the Lithuanian balance beam world championships with Koo Koo Kakootchna from Lithuania third.
Irv
Did you finish up with your standard trick, the three of you doing the front running back 1½ with 2½ full twists?
Nancy
Yeah! We pulled that one off with no contest!
Roy
That must have been something to see.
Irv
Is there anything else going on?

Nancy
Roy and I got engaged!
Irv
Engaged? Roy, you didn't tell me that!
Roy
Yeah! We stopped off at San Juan Capistrano and made arrangements to get married the first day of summer, 2023. Isn't that a corker?
Irv
They've got some strange swallows in San Juan Capistrano, don't they?
Roy
Yes! Every fall the swallows fly 6,000 miles to Argentina, stay until March, and then fly back to their home on the Capistrano Coast.
Irv
Doesn't that cause a strange bug to fly out of your nostril?
Roy
It sure does! Now a similar theme upon which I never seem to tire called *Remembrances of My Father.*

Remembrances of My Father

When a cat died, he'd put it in a hole in the ground and plant a tree over it, and say, *"The cat will make good fertilizer."*

My dad loved plants and worked in his garden. When a plant was doing well, he'd be proud and exclaim his joy. When a plant refused to grow, he'd yank it out and throw it away. He only had time for plants that showed promise.

My dad said, *"See what I'm doing?"* Yes, I'd say. Polishing your shoes. *"Do you see where I'm polishing?"* Yes. The back. The lesson was that the whole shoe needed to be polished, not just the part seen by others.

My dad said, *"When you're working for somebody else, give 'em an extra half hour. You'll always have a job"*.

Irv
Well! That elucidation is a little more reasonable.
Roy
My dad didn't say much, but what he said could have come from a bible.
Irv
When I think of myself dying, I think kindly of my Dad putting me in a hole under a tree so I'll make good fertilizer.
Roy
At least you're not wasted. *Ha! Ha! Ha!* I felt my father had time for people who would grow.
Irv
And you were right!
Roy
And that it was important to take care of all of me rather that just the portion that shows.
Irv
Where was he wrong in that?

Roy
That if I gave a little extra, I would always be needed.
Irv
Where could I fault him?

There is so much more!

My middle daughter, Lili, says, *"Your experience isn't the center of everything, because there are so many other living beings out there experiencing life other than you."* But there are no other individuals existing in the Universe exactly like you, whether or not they have the ability to be aware of the Universe. I like to say once we know we're here on Earth, it's a truism.

The point is: without you being alive with awareness there is no Universe. You, being alive and aware is the only reason the Universe exists. Those who are not aware of the Universe means for them the Universe doesn't exist. Isn't that sort of curious? You could say the Universe exists only to those who are aware of it.

Roy
Another way to put it is the Universe exists only when you're aware it does.
Irv
Does that mean the Universe doesn't exist if you're blind?
Roy
Don't be stupid!

From Lili's Last Letter:
Lili asks; Is it important to you to retain a sense of your individual self after leaving your body, and if so, why?
I can't think of any good reason. That reminds me, Tom asked that when I died, if I'd send him a message from the dead to let him know I was still part of life after death.
I agreed, *"Sure! Why not?"* But what's the net result?
In the future he gets my message and, sure enough, somehow Doug's still around.

Then, if the living can communicate with the dead, why couldn't he ask me questions? *(Question: When dead, if I can communicate to the living, can the living communicate back?)*

Tom says, *"Hey, Doug, What's it like being dead?"*

Well, I'd go into a long harangue. Well, we have no head or extremities, or five senses. We have feelings! We feel great!

Tom would ask, *"Where are the feelings?"*

I'd say, *"They are sort of in the air."*

Tom would say, *"You have no place for feelings?"*

I'd say, *"It's tough to explain. You'd have to be here."*

He'd ask me, *"Is there any sex? Are you going to recreate life?"*

I'd say, *"No! There's nothing like that here on the other side."*

Tom would say, *"Are there any hamburger sandwiches or malted milk?"*

I'd say, *"No! No! No! Nothing like that!"*

And so on and so on!

Roy
I don't know where to go with a conversation like this.
Irv
You get no mental picture of life after death?
Roy
No! I don't! While looking for an essay to make this book over 200 pages, I ran into this dream.
Irv
I keep asking you is this a dream journal?
Roy
It's a dream about my own death. I could probably have justified placing this dream at the end of the book, but then after some thought; I decided to put *Black Clouds and Lightning* here in a less disheartening place.

Black Clouds and Lightning

I sleep in a bed next to a window whose mattress height is exactly that of the sill. *(In the past, rain has splashed on the sill as I contentedly like feeling the fine, light, cooling spray on my face.)* It was four in the morning and I had many covers and was probably too warm. My eyes were gentle and decisive in their flickering while I was in deep REM sleep. We'd seen a movie the night before with Kim Basinger, who played an alien from another planet. The movie included a scene with the tiny principal actors climbing atop a huge satellite receiver in a heavy rainstorm that was being successively hit with lightning. This scene was not the basis for the dream, but probably the trigger for the dreams method. As most dreams do, it portrayed this time in my life and my general state of mind. A looming cloud with lightning is similar to infrequent previous dreams. They're probably are about death.

In this dream, I live in a hillside house and I'm comfortably resting late one morning in bed. I can see the outside clearly for the room has a large sliding glass door overlooking a stretch of lawn and beyond, a beautiful view. My spouse is with me but in this dream, but it isn't important. I'm suddenly aware of an immense dark, black cloud quickly approaching from over the distant ocean and am fascinated by this event and walk outside to more closely witness this rare phenomenon. Then the cloud looms large and unbearably close to me and perhaps as high as the housetop. It blocks the sun, is pitch black and curling slowly, and it seems, focused particularly on me. It casts threatening shadows. Its significant granular texture is quietly moving, thick and disturbing. It suggests black and gaseous twisting hair, deliberately and consciously swirling like soot. If I breathed it, I'd choke.

Nevertheless, I'm fascinated, and for a more intense experience, I run beneath the cloud which is now no higher than a few feet above me extending off into the sky. Then I become wary as I realize the cloud will generate a lightning strike. I or anyone standing would become a deadly conduit, and I caution my friends (for now I have a friends) to follow my action by laying down. I lie beneath the menacing cloud and hope the decision for friends and myself will keep us safe. But then I see transparent, almost invisible lines projecting from the bottom of the cloud bottom to the Earth that I interpret as the preliminary signal for a lightning strike. I signal my friends to get up and run, and we scamper 60 or so yards away and turn to watch the house and black cloud.

Four short, powerful lightning strikes, perhaps each with a diameter of four feet, emanated at once from the bottom of the clouds striking the bottoms of four immense, thickly trunked pine trees. All four burst into flame with fiery tongues leaping on each side along vertical openings in the bark. The huge tree second from the right cracks and explodes at its base and the entire, immense tree crumples in a mindshattering fall and thunders to the ground - at which time, I awake.

Meaning:

I am comfortable in my house.
   (I am comfortable in my present life.)
I see a fascinating, but ominous dark cloud approaching.
   (I see a fascinating, but ominous death approaching.)
I make motions to escape by running away from approaching disaster.
   (I eat and exercise properly to delay death and do pleasing things in spare time.)
Disaster strikes four trees.
   (A disaster befalls my three children and me who are

represented by the four trees.
One tree crumples in final destruction.
(I crumple in final destruction (die), because I'm older and do not have my children's time to live.)
The other three trees burst into flame, but are not toppled.
(The other three trees symbolizing my three children are injured by the fourth crumbling, which is a sign off my own death, but the children will survive.)

The dream is about my inevitable death as it relates to my three children and me. Right now, I feel pretty good.

Roy
When death stops the *living kind* of living in the fresh air and fields it also begins in the *dead kind* of living in the grave or field. The body deteriorates, the skin shrivels, shrinks and shreds. The bones mellow, darken and begin to disappear. The nerves, veins and arteries convert to detritus and the remaining essence becomes energy for a new type of life, such as worms, toads, grasshoppers, etc. Is that a good enough description? So I'd say, definitely, yes. One type of life really leads to another type of life.
Do you understand what I'm trying to tell you?
Irv
No!
Roy
OK, then, on the subject of religion. What's more important than religion?

On the Subject of Religion

My contractor friend and his wife were raised by Mormons, continued in the Mormon faith and have raised their children as Mormons. I have a beloved client who had Catholic parents. She continued in the Catholic faith and raised her seven kids Catholic. One of my oldest friends had parents who were devoted to the Christian Science religion, and my friend became a Christian Scientist and raised his children in the same faith. By my experience, it seems the religion of the parents is passed down to the children who then pass it down to their own children. This is how traditions are made.

Small children, unable to fend for themselves, are dependent on their parents for survival. Without the love and caring parents devote to their children, they'd die. If they want to be raised in peace and harmony, children, who have no choice in their immediate family are forced to, must, and usually want to comply with the wishes of their elders. What the parents know and believe has a critical influence on the life of a child, including what the child knows and how he or she deals with life. Before the age of ten, a child must respond and conform to the messages it hears from the parents. If he or she doesn't, the penalty is huge, for he or she is not liked, or in the worst case, may be abused or abandoned.

Therefore it's reasonable to expect that grown-up children, that is, those who are old enough to be marriageable, having successfully navigated their days of dependency, will know and believe something very similar to those of their parents, and since their parents' belief has already been determined and they've not been exposed to other religions or other ways of knowing and living life, will raise their own children in the only way they know how, with the same beliefs as their parents, which becomes the child's own. Never was it so true, that what *goes around, comes around.* What continues becomes traditional and in most cases, whatever religion a child learns, he teaches.

Looking at my own life, I've noticed I have no church-going religion. It's only after being exposed to people who regularly go to church that I've come to ask myself why *I* don't have a religion and go to church? Though I don't belong to a church, I do have powerful enthusiasms and passionate philosophies, and don't look or especially feel different from most everyone else. I've functioned in a lasting business for well over 50 years, and I'm certainly religious when it comes to caring about my self and caring about my family and work. Do I, or do I not have a religion? I decided to ask myself how *I* was raised. The answer to that question might let me know what I believe and how I differ, if I do, from my religious and church-going friends. It seemed an act of common sense to look into my own childhood and see how *I* was raised and how *I* came to *my* beliefs and, following what seems to be the normal rule, how I would raise *my own* children. If I do that, I am asking myself about my parents' religion and my grandparents' religion, or lack of a religion, to determine how I was raised and to discover my beliefs and my own religion.

Let me say right at the beginning, I have some strong beliefs about humanity and the world. To illustrate what I think, I'd like to use the words of Henry James written in letters to his sons:

"*Every man who has reached his intellectual teens begins to suspect that life is no farce; that it is not a genteel comedy ever; that it flowers and fructifies out of the profoundest tragic depths of the essential dearth in* which its roots are plunged. The natural inheritance of everyone who is capable of spiritual life is an un-subdued forest where the wolf howls and the obscene bird of night chatters."

Beginnings

In the furnace room when I was six years old, trying to get a small box open, my father said to my mother, *"Mother, let Doug do it alone, he can figure it out for himself."* This phrase planted the seed in my brain that *"I could figure things out for myself."* Later, trying to manipulate a hammer and nail, my father said, *"Use your ingenuity."* Again my dad planted the seed that possibly I had something called *"ingenuity."* While that was running through my mind, I remember another time when he said, *"Use your common sense."* Evidently, I also had something within me called *"common sense."* I began to suspect *I could figure things out for myself using ingenuity and common sense.* Thereafter, I suspected I had a religion of common sense.

The Religion of Common Sense

The eldest of seven, my father was forced to quit school in the middle of seventh grade and go to work to help raise a family of nine. As a child, my dad had no religion and attended no services, but always used the word, *"Lord"* with reverence and respect. He looked kindly on all people whether they went to church or not.

My mother's mother was a devout Catholic who attended services regularly. My mother's father was a brilliant journalist and editor, who believed, along with his colleagues, Mark Twain, Jack London, Marcel Proust, Bertrand Russell and H. L. Mencken, in atheism. As the eldest child with a strong literary bent and *"Daddy's little girl,"* my mother leaned heavily toward her dad's belief in atheism.

My four-years-younger brother, Dave, and I were neither prevented from nor encouraged to go to church, nor was there any opportunity to attend church services since nobody went. We were raised by my father who had no formal education, but was respectful of all religions, and my mother who was at heart an atheist with an acceptance of all people and regard for all religions.

Common Sense Religion – Three Parts

The habit of attending religious ceremonies and obtaining a religious education are usually one of the earliest of American experiences. From my early life I seem to have just three pieces of knowledge that affected my grown-up life: (1) *Figuring things out for myself;* (2) *using ingenuity; and* (3) *common sense* worked together with these to form my lifetime religion.

Figuring things out for myself while using my ingenuity required special talents. Whether I had those or not, I did not know. But using common sense was something I thought I understood.

Of course, using *"common sense"* involved other qualities like reasonableness, understanding, and empathy and open mind. Evidently, I had to have some of those, too. If touching a hot frying pan with my finger would burn me, then I shouldn't do that. If jumping off a cliff might cause me to break a leg, I shouldn't do that. If crossing the double line while driving might get me and travelers killed, I shouldn't do that.

I'm not a Christian Scientist, Mormon, Catholic, Protestant, Muslim, Jew, Hindu or Buddhist. My religion is one some might think too simple. It's called the *"Religion of Common Sense,"* which, to me, means *"figuring things out for myself using my ingenuity and common sense."*

Commandments
Even without having religious training, I did live my life adhering to the Ten Commandments. The Ten Commandments are: *having no other God before the theoretical "only one"; making no carved images of what I think God might look like; not taking God's name in vain; remembering to relax and pray on Sunday; honoring mom and dad; committing no murder, adultery, or robbery, or bearing false witness, or coveting another's wife.*

Well, I should say I *"almost"* lived by the Ten Commandments. While yet immature and having made a major error, I got divorced and remarried someone who'd made the same mistake. I corrected mine. It was necessary she correct hers.

Ten Commandments
What follows is my analysis of the Ten Commandments.

1 Thou shalt have no other Gods before me. *If God is the Universal Force, I have no other God.*

2 Thou shalt make no carved images. *It's hard to make a carving of the Universal Force. It's already pretty well been carved by people's thoughts.*

3 Thou shalt not take the Lord's name in vain. *Because the Universal force is incapable of caring, it makes little difference to swear in its name.*

4 Thou shalt remember the Sabbath day. *What is the Universal Force's Sabbath day? The day the Universe was born, the big bang day, 13 billion years ago? I wasn't there and only know what I think is the best of what's known.*

5 Thou shalt honor thy father and mother. *Fortunately, I had by all good standards, outstanding parents, and shall always honor them.*

6 Thou shalt commit no murder. *This is ridiculous! I don't need to pray not to kill somebody. It's the last thing on my mind, but it depends on circumstances. If someone injures my kid, I'll not be responsible for what I'll do. This is a human thing. Sometimes murder is a human species thing, such as if my family is threatened, I will defend it and do what I feel needs to be done.*

7 Thou shalt not commit adultery. *I've got to bend on that one. In my first marriage of 25 years, I made lifetime commitments far before I was emotionally ready. In my new marriage, we've had over 34 years of wedded bliss, caring for seven children and eight grandchildren, all justified by correcting a bad mistake.*

8 Thou shalt not steal. *What's there to steal? If you were ready to die from lack of food and water, I'd say OK; perhaps I'd be more lenient. I'm a fortunate man. I've got a good wife and good kids and plenty at stake to make a serious decision about what to do next.*

9 Thou shalt not bear false witness. *I've had false witness borne against me. It's not pretty. I'd never do that to someone else. How does that fit with "Do unto others as you would have them do unto you?" Bearing false witness blackens both names.*

10 Thou shalt not covet thy neighbor's wife. *I have to give that one a mea culpa because I did and my new wife coveted another's husband. Eventually everyone was happier including the soon-to-be unmarried spouses. Where is it written, "Thou shalt not learn from one's mistakes."?*

Now I'd like to interpret a prayer my mother taught me as a child.

"*Now I lay me down to sleep,
I pray the Lord my soul to keep,*

*If I should die before I wake,
I pray the Lord my soul to take."*

Interpretation:

Line 1 - I'm being put to bed.
Line 2 – Even though I've just begun my life, I'm praying or asking or hoping that some powerful personage that I don't know will keep my soul for me, if I have a soul, because, evidently I couldn't keep it myself and mom and dad evidently aren't up to it.
Line 3 – I speculate about dying before morning even though mom and dad thought I'd probably make it through the night. At that time, death at 6 years old was far beyond my imagination.
Line 4 - I was encouraged to verbalize that it was my prayer, hope, desire that *IF*, as a youngster, I were to pass on to a better world, the powerful personage whom I don't know would accept my soul, which I was not sure what one was or if I had one, and keep it, presumably, in a better place than it already was.

Prayer allows the one who prays to clarify his subject. It is similar to hope, but more important because it's also a verbalized medium of expression. It can be intimate, or altruistic, or selfish, or desperate. But in every case it clarifies the thoughts, feelings and position of the one who prays, and more firmly establishes that persons wants and desires that more easily provoke an action to achieve a desired end.

It is certain that it is beneficial in the majority of cases, that if the ill, injured, or unhappy person knows he or she is being prayed for, he or she knows those praying persons care for them and knowing they are cared for, to whatever degree encourages self worth and a greater ability to cure themselves. I can't imagine a prayer to another or the self that is hoping, wishing or desiring of a positive outcome, not being extremely beneficial to whomever is being prayed for.

More Commandments

I think there should be more than Ten Commandments, because the new ones would be vital to all planet life and make the core of my personal religion, *Common Sense.*

A simple analysis: The Earth is the mother of all living things that have been on it, and are on it along with ebola, and AIDS. If the Earth is mother, then like every other living thing that has a mother, every living thing is an only child or sibling. In that case killing any living thing could be like killing a brother, sister, father, mother or close relative. Of course, if we are permitted to be born and live on Earth, it is under the condition that eating meat forces killing. Check with our digestive system if you don't belive it. Don't kill the messenger. I'd like to be wrong. There are Ten Commandments, shouldn't there be more? How about:

(11) *Learn from your mistakes.*

(12) *Do unto all living things as you would have them do unto you.*

Of course, look inside our stomachs. Man is an omnivore, a species designed to eat both meat and vegetables. As a whole, by the make of his alimentary tract, human creatures are unalterably constructed to eat meat as well as vegetables. We are stuck with it and can't get off! *(Is this condition number one?)*

Man as a Species

Common sense tells me that man, like the lion, tiger and bear, is a *species*. Almost all animal species have two eyes, two legs, two arms, one head, two eyes, two ears, one nose and one method of procreation. Though endowed with mankind's essentials, our species has different personalized qualities. There is no other animal better than mankind at remembering the past and speculating on the future. In my opinion, humans don't possess any special favors like when we die, living again in heaven. I believe the following: *"In a single tick of the cosmic clock, I'm stratum."*

In figuring things out by using my ingenuity and common sense, there is no evidence for heaven. To me, the idea of belief is not substantial enough to answer such an important question. In the Common Sense religion, when a member of a species dies, except in memory, that particular example is gone! The party's over! I've seen road kill and human fossils in ancient strata. They have not returned.

Nature, however, has specifically designed us to eat meat. It defies the religion of Common Sense to battle such a specific reality. If another animal needed meat, or me for sustenance, I'd want him to be swift and gentle about what he's going to do, and then clean up whatever mess he's made. Shouldn't we be as empathetic regarding animals we eat?

What about curiosity? Shouldn't there be a Commandment such as number 13?

(13) *"Thou shalt investigate and explore everything of which you are capable."* Mankind does that anyway. In fact, he's paranoid about it. What with a 26-mile cyclotron to explore stars and the universe, a permanent space station

and the newer telescopes, the internet, and nuclear energy, we're certainly making stupendous strides in exploring and investigating everything of which we are capable. I can't imagine a commandment like, *"For even greater knowledge, thou shalt not use all of mankind's explorative abilities."* Like procreation, we humans are going to do it anyway.

(14) *"Thou shalt look inward to examine yourself to see if your motives make the world a happier or less happy place."*

That's a heavy one. It means I have to look at what, where and why I do what I do before I do it. It's *"common sense"* and the rule is *think before I do.*

(15) *"Understand the Whole"*
In my *Common Sense* religion, it is necessary for me to understand the *whole* because *"what I think"* involves the *whole* even if I don't know the whole. How can the whole *not* influence what I *(or we)* think?

It's not my intention to include petty thoughts that bore you *(or me)*, but I've tried to pick the essentials of *"what I think"* so a more complete understanding will occur to each of us.

I came to thinking in terms of the *"whole"* through my 54-year career as an architect doing new homes and remodeling in Malibu. To be a good architect, I need to *"get the whole picture,"* The owner doesn't have the whole picture; he says, *"I just want a house."*

1 – The contractor says, *"Show me what to build and I'll build it."*

2 – The bureaucratic agencies have rules to be followed and stamped; they say, *"Show me what you propose, and we'll stamp it if it's allowed."*

3 – The site says I contain certain elements, direction, wind, terrain, water, freezing, vegetation, slope, etc., and says, *Though I speak not, do the best with all my requirements:* water table, shape of terrain, wind direction, etc.

4 – As the designer, I have my own sense of art and process and must pay attention to my own life's integrity and so I say, *"I must know the whole, but that includes how I want to live my life."*

As a group in process, these essential considerations are the *whole* that must happily emerge inside the new creation. If others don't get the whole, who get's it? It has to be me, the architect. That's why I get the big bucks.

I have to know all the ins and outs of each of the four divisions, and keep everyone smiling to produce a life work of which I'm proud. As it turns out, buildings are built by people, therefore, if I'm the main person, what the building is, is a reflection of me and who I am. Who I am looks back at me as the finished building. To produce something of which I'm proud involves imagination, sensitivity to the owner and environment, the cost of the project, and whether the owners and I can agree for a couple of years on what we're doing.

Because there are many solutions to a problem, I like to think in scenarios. I often say, *"Let's list all the different ways we can meet the purpose, put them on the table, and then choose one."* This usually works because everyone gets a say and a joint solution is usually agreeable.

Therefore, I have included seeing the whole in my views of my life. Of course, no one can ever get the whole picture. It's too big, too miraculous, too astounding, but it's my intention to understand it to the degree of my capability. Perhaps another commandment I might add is *"Thou shalt understand the whole of the universe to the best of your capability."*

Greatest Adventures

Socrates is supposed to have said; all he really *"knew"* was the extent of his own ignorance. Christopher Hitchens comments about this in his own book, *"This to me is still the definition of an educated person."* It means, then, if we subtract a person's ignorance, what's left over is either nothing or his education.

In the religion of Common Sense, I have chosen my own piece of philosophy, *"The greatest adventures lie within the realm of my own ignorance."* New knowledge, then, is the great adventure; optimistic in resolve, educational in spirit.

Keeping an open mind allows both pleasant and unpleasant things to enter, and that means my experience of life is broadened. A broadened experience of life means I know more, have felt more feelings, and have had more thought-provoking ideas leading me to a greater depth in creativity, and a life that is richer, more fulfilling and complete.

Knowing and Believing

I *know* an open mind is better than a closed mind. How do I know? I'm in great sympathy with the late Dr. David Viscott's definition of *knowing*. *"Knowing is the truth from a certain perspective."* So, I *do* know things. But what I *know* is what I *believe*. My definition of belief is also Dr. Viscott's definition; that belief is *"knowing something is so, whether or not it is."*

To me, knowing is strongly related to *faith, confidence,* and *truth*. I know the sun will come up because it comes up every day for my lifetime. Therefore, I have *faith* it will come up. I have *confidence* it will come up. And this *faith* and *confidence* adds up to my *truth*, and the truth is, *"The sun will come up."* To me, faith must be based on a percentage of past performance. Faith based on no past performance is blind faith.

(There are nine more pages on the way to a full statement on what I'm all about at the age of 87. To be completed I don't know when.)

A Percentage Kind of a Guy

Faith, being a condition where I can have a lot of faith, or have a moderate amount of faith, or hardly any faith, is a matter of percentages. If I eat, my hunger is assuaged. If I drink, my thirst is assuaged. If I work hard at something, I love that people will pay me and, hence, give me a place to live, have a family, and complete my life. I have faith it will rain during the rainy season, or snow during winter, or be hot in the sand in summer. Of course, the sun coming up every day is one thing of which I'm completely certain. Faith, for me, depends on percentages. I had faith it would rain during the rainy season for two years. It did not. Sometimes I can be disappointed in my faith. Unless it's like the sun coming up, faith is chancy, and for me depends on what it did in the past.

People are Different

People are as different as fingerprints. What one person

knows and believes is different from what another person knows and believes. Even in the same family, the father has one system of beliefs, *"knowing something is so, whether or not it is,"* and things he knows, which is *"The truth from his perspective."* The mother has another system of beliefs, *"knowing something is so, whether or not it is,"* and things she knows, which is *"The truth from her perspective."*

Following Parents' Beliefs
Each person, male or female, is born at a different time when the Earth has spun an additional nine months on its axis, and time, moving in a straight line as it does, is nine months or so in advance from where it was before. Each new baby born at each new time has its own qualities of mind, body, spirit and soul, including an arbitrary combination of their parent's mind, body and soul. *Each soul and spirit is, then, unique and inviolable.* I believe a soul must have a body. I don't believe a soul can exist in another dimension or after its body is dead. I do believe a soul can be remembered, but lost when the one who remembers dies. Regarding the human species, I believe, if desired, a soul can be imagined for any singular piece of matter, rocks, water, fire, gas, etc., in the Universe.

Beginning of the World
In the very beginning, the unimaginable happened! A tiny *nothing* exploded and developed into an unimaginably large number of energy and particles and other stuff that eventually became light, electro-magnetic forces, etc. and other things likely only to be read about in science magazines.

Over billions of years, that energy made an unimaginable number of galaxies, black holes, giant dwarfs, etc., one of which is our average-sized Milky Way galaxy still expanding and moving out into space along with our solar system. It has our sun and eight rotating planets, including Earth, and contains various moons.

Four billion years after our universe was born, grass began to grow, encouraging oxygen to form and be released into the atmosphere. Oxygen in the air was the major element depended upon to produce all life. Slowly, fish, lizards, birds, reptiles and tiny mammals inhabited the Earth, culminating in dinosaurs, masters of the planet for well over 135 million years.

Then, 66 million years ago, a comet, six miles in diameter, struck the Yucatan Peninsula, creating a black cloud that enveloped Earth, darkening, freezing and terminating the life of dinosaurs and most everything on our planet. It caused our fifth extinction, wiping out 80% of all the plants and animals on Earth.

Sixty-four million years passed before warm-blooded animals developed to take the place of dinosaurs, and about 100,000 years ago, a primitive creature arrived resembling man. For 90,000 years, mankind lived in tribes, killing other living creatures for food. After the ice age 11,000 years ago, and after large animals had been hunted to extinction, man discovered he could keep domestic animals and eat plants for food. Catching and eating wild creatures became less important, because man was able to survive the lean years and winter due to eating birds, animals and vegetables he'd grown and stored.

Earth is one of the byproducts of the big bang. Considering everything, Earth *is* our Mother. I live on Mother Earth! In the religion of Common Sense with Earth as the mother and the big bang the father, everything living or non-living on Earth is my sister or brother. I'd like to take it a step farther and say, even if I eat animals, they should be treated lovingly and appreciatively!

Process and Context

I believe what is to be accomplished today should be in the context of what's happening today. Certainly, what happened yesterday is already recorded for yesterday. The alternative *(recreating the past)* is a waste of time. To build an aircraft using yesterday's methods is ridiculous and doesn't meet the criteria of gained knowledge and common sense. Why not use the new, the tested, and the best that's available? Intelligence and common sense gives us the opportunity to use only the latest proven methods to produce a transportation system that flies through the air with the greatest of ease, allowing minimum fuel use and advanced speed. Certainly, I wouldn't want to buy a ten-year-old car or fly in a thirty-year-old plane or travel in a train of the 1920s. Not to be up-to-date is a negative mark against the progress and miracle of mankind.

Time and Reality

Any time I snap my fingers, through all time and distance, I capture instant reality. It's a waste of creativity and intelligence to demand today the reality of a former time. When someone snapped their fingers and asked who would be more mature, a 20-year old or an 8-year old, expecting I'd say the elder. My answer was that they'd both be mature for their age. Others have said and I agree that, *"when I was a child, I thought like a child; when I was a young adult, I thought as a young adult; when I was an old man, I thought as an old man."* Of course, I've known some young people with greater maturity than their older friends, all attesting to the fact that all people are distinctly unique.

(It makes me unhappy to say to a large degree, the computer age has passed me by.)

Correct me if I'm Wrong

In any discussion I may have on my philosophy of religion and of life on earth, it's good for me to continue my completed comments with a word directed to any thinking listener: *"Correct me if I'm wrong."* If the comment remains unanswered, I'll assume tentative agreement and continue with my argument. If a colleague corrects me, I'm personally bound to listen carefully and agree or not agree. I might learn something new, and correct my thinking. The worst that can happen is that whatever I've said will be more fully rounded out and better understood by both of us.

The Brain is a Tool

To understand my personal *Common Sense* religion, it's important to know the viewpoint I take when I observe the world. Whether a religion or my personal life philosophy, my own way of seeing things must view the whole picture. Viewing only a part of the picture allows me to remain in doubt as to what I might have missed.

Anyway, *the greatest adventures lie within the realm of my own ignorance.* One such viewpoint is the difference between the brain and the self. It turns out the brain is not the self. It's not where I live. The eye is a tool. The ear, the nose, the skin, the tongue are tools. The body is a tool. It runs, it works, it plays, it propagates. I have to ask myself, where's the seat of the soul? Is it the toe, the navel, the center of the brain, the elbow, or the buttocks? Choose any place and there I'll be. The lines of communication are nerves that travel in spidery webs through the entire body, carrying signals, sometimes from the great unconscious mind. *(Who can understand the interweaving complexities of human make-up?)* The brain is the clearinghouse for messages. It's the meter box or main panel. It's hooked to the power source, but it's not the power source. The brain is a tool that can be used by the self to get what it needs for fulfillment or achievement. The brain is the manager of the company. Its job is to implement the needs of the self.

Sometimes the messages received by the brain are not clear and difficult to decipher. Two or more messages, understood to be right or wrong but initiated by the self, confuse the brain, leading to conflict in the whole organism. If the self, the captain, the spirit of the inner person is deluded, it may result in excess smoking, drinking, drugs, food or lack thereof, or other deleterious affects. A muddled self is a contributing factor to headaches, backaches, eczema, ulcers, rashes and high blood pressure. Unsolved, conflicting messages allows the organism to wither and break. The spirit is short-circuited and loss of power occurs.

I See the World This Way

The religion of *Common Sense* must encompass the whole universe and especially our entire world, since our one planet *(off of which, we shall not get)* is the mother of all life and all living creations. They are our siblings and demand to be treated as such.

Between Venus and Mars, Earth swirls around the sun, while at the same time, rotates around itself at the equator at the rate of about 1,000 miles an hour. This rapid movement of our planet, which on the surface is made up of 70% water and 30% land, energizes our atmosphere, causing winds, rains, tornadoes, hurricanes, fog, and dust storms. The Earth, a metal-based planet *(as opposed to a gas-based planet like Saturn, Jupiter or Uranus),* is halfway through its 9-billion year existence. It has a molten core of lead boiling away at its center that regularly spouts volcanoes, spewing tons of carbon dioxide as well as life-enhancing minerals into the oceans and atmosphere. If a volcano spews forth beneath the ocean, it may precipitate a tsunami causing huge waves that devastate shorelines. The perpetual rotation also forces powerful oceanic currents to curl and twist in slightly changing patterns around projecting islands and landforms.

Our life-giving atmosphere is made of an extremely thin layer of air compared to the size of the earth. It consists of 78 percent nitrogen and 21 percent oxygen. The habitable space for all living things is well below that of the world's highest mountain at 29,000 feet. Twelve thousand feet above sea level is the highest anyone might safely travel without blacking out. Average timberlines are 10,000 feet below the highest mountains. Life is compelled to adapt to these unasked for, but persistent and continuing facts and forces. We are truly the offspring of our miraculous Mother. Seen from space, this tiny, brilliant, watery-blue ball with its large, white, circling moon is alone and lost and singular in the surrounding black vastness of space, and we're on it in the dark. We can't get off! We're on this miraculous terrarium until we die, and our bones will remain until about 4 billion years when the heat of a dying sun swallows our planet.

Self

If the *Self* is not *"I,"* it's certainly not anyone else. Without the tools of my organism, my self does not exist. But, with the full senses of my organism, I occupy the most significant place in my world. My tools send messages back to me, and I feel myself feeling which is my calling. I feel everything. I feel sad. I feel angry. I feel anxious. I feel loving. I feel joyous. I can feel these things singly or all at once. With my tools I can have multiple feelings. I can feel lonely and in love. I can feel sad and yet grateful. I can feel fearful, yet hopeful. I like to feel good. I don't like to feel bad. My organism knows which is which, though I cannot speak to it, though when I tell it, it's not in words. When I feel good, I instruct my organism to continue to do something to make me feel good again.

I control my organism, but like anything mechanical, things sometimes go wrong. Should I burn my hand, my organism hurts and tells me. I can feel foolish or stupid or regretful or angry or a combination of all my feelings depending on my attitude. Oh, yes! I have an attitude! An attitude is the average state of feelings depending on a conglomeration of feelings and processing of incoming messages, *Self* begs the questions, how did life start or when was the beginning of consciousness? What inspired the first living organism to move, to spawn and to replicate? By the use of figuring it out for myself with ingenuity and common sense and after all the reading I've done, both in the religious scriptures and the scientific literature, I have to say I haven't the faintest idea.

Irv
Where does all that philosophizing leave you?

Roy
Everywhere and nowhere.
Irv
What are you going to do about that?
Roy
What does the self, need? It needs only that which can be defined by the Earth's atmosphere, its only home.
Irv
Not much to do, eh?
Roy
Any *"Self"* either continues living or decides not to, which requires suicide.
Irv
So if you like life, go on living. If you don't like life, figure out how to die.
Roy
It's not an easy choice, though certainly elementary my dear Watson!
Irv
Don't you have anything nicer to tell me than that?
Roy
Yes I do! Nancy and I are getting married on the first day of summer, June 21, 2023.
Irv
Wow! That's great! Will the swallows come back to Capistrano in time for the wedding?
Roy
They'll be back for the in celebration freely tweeting three of Brahms Classic Love Songs.

END

About the Author

Born in Elmhurst, a suburb of Chicago, Doug was educated at the University of Illinois in Champaign-Urbana. In 1955 he built his first house in Santa Monica Canyon, California, and in the following years his wife gave birth to three marvelous daughters. By January of 1958 he became the first permanent architect doing business solely in Malibu. In 1966 he moved his family into a new Malibu architect's dream home overlooking Surfrider Beach. Five years later it burned to the ground and it took him two more years to build a more fire-resistant house over the same foundations. The new house remains noted in Gebhardt and Winter's, Los Angeles Guide to Architecture. In 1964 Doug did a contemporary house for Jack Hogan later to be sold to Muriel Kessler and her husband, who lived in it for 47 years before selling it to Chris and Susanna Caparro. Chris noted the quality of the house and alerted the Cultural Heritage Commission of the City of Los Angeles. It was quickly selected in the Modern Style and classified as a Cultural Historical Monument No. 1152. In June of 2022 it was placed on the National Register of Historical Places by the United States Department of the Interior.

Doug has spent most of his career doing new houses and additions in Malibu and local areas, but has also designed and built single jobs in Kauai, Greece, Denver, Fallbrook, Barstow, Long Beach, New York and eight projects in Santa Barbara. In 1980 he was divorced from his first wife and for many years was married to Marge Lewi-Rucker who had four children of her own. All are grown up along with Doug's three and are passionately invested in their own lives. Marge is deceased and Doug now lives content in a small house of his own design on a landscaped acre of property in the mountains above Malibu, Retired from architecture, he brings a special passion to writing and photographic digital art.

Other Books by Doug Rucker

Personal Journey
>*Poems predicting next phase of life*

Early Stories
>*Autobiography – Birth through university*

Groundwork
>*Autobiography – Marriage to office opening*

Growing Edge
>*Autobiography – Office opening to rec complex*

Moving Through
>*Collection of poems with "No Think" pastels*

Book of Words
>*Essay collection – Humor & philosophy*

Harold and the Acid Sea of Reality
>*Thoughts on fantasy & reality*

Trial by Fire – A Tale of Two Houses
>*Burning and rebuilding of home*

Building a Home that Loves You
>*Philosophy of architecture with pictures*

Transitions
>*Realism, Reflections Abstract & comments*

Thinking in the Abstract
>*Deciphering abstract art*

No Think Drawings
>*Unplaned drawings revealing the subconscious*

Poetries
>*Abstract art, poetry, & prose*

Catchall
>*60 essays on ideas and beliefs*

www.ingramcontent.com/pod-product-compliance
Lightning Source LLC
Chambersburg PA
CBHW040801150426
42811CB00056B/1128